Whose Constitution

AN INQUIRY INTO THE
GENERAL WELFARE

THERE IS *an American solution for American national problems if we approach them in the spirit of the men who called the Constitutional Convention and obtained, by their brilliant advocacy of the national approach, the adoption of the Constitution by the thirteen confederated States.*

Whose Constitution?

AN INQUIRY INTO THE GENERAL WELFARE

BY

HENRY A. WALLACE

GREENWOOD PRESS, PUBLISHERS
WESTPORT, CONNECTICUT

1597835

Contents

Part Three
We The People

Part Four
Democracy in Action

Introduction

THERE has continually flamed in the heart of America the belief that this continent was different. On this new soil mankind would escape from the compulsions, the suspicions and the greeds of the Old World. Americans, whether living in the United States, or in the 20 sister republics or the Dominion of Canada felt that the New World had in it the call of destiny toward a higher standard of living and a more universal distribution of happiness. The American faith has been a rather simple one and in some ways rather childlike. Nevertheless, the American faith is real, glorious, powerful, and, in my opinion, remains a real hope of the world's future.

In the United States the New World faith found its first powerful written manifestation in the Declaration of Independence and its second in the preamble to the Constitution. The two documents set the poles between which the spirit of the New World continually oscillates. In the Declaration of Independence we find expressed in rather extreme form the doctrine of individual liberty, impatience with restraint, and the expression of the right of revolution. But the spirit of liberty and independence can be carried too far and twelve years after the Declaration of Independence we find set forth the doctrine of unity and interdependence, the will of a sovereign people in the familiar words:

"We the people of the United States, in order to form a more perfect union, establish justice, insure domestic tranquillity, provide for the common defense, promote the general welfare and secure the blessings of liberty to ourselves and our posterity, do ordain and establish this Constitution."

In the spirit both of the Declaration and of this preamble the people of the United States subdued the forests, plowed the fields, built the roads, peopled the land all the way to the Pacific and set the wheels of a myriad of factories humming. At times the individualistic spirit of the Declaration dominated the people's feelings and at times the spirit of the preamble dominated. To Jackson's toast, "Our federal union, it must be preserved!" there was always Calhoun's reply, "The Union, *next to our liberty*, most dear!" Again and again there were quarrels and setbacks. But always in case of need the inmost soul of the American people seemed to respond to the fiat: "We the people of the United States, in order to form a more perfect union." And always when small and narrow men endeavored to prostitute the powers of government for the selfish needs of particular classes, there came a time when governmental powers were used from the standpoint of justice and the general welfare.

There are those who say that the United States is now about ready to follow the same path as has been followed in the Old World. Some even say that the spirit of the United States is less ready to face the problems of a mature nation than the spirit of Europe. It is said that we have been lucky in having such a thin population relative to huge natural resources. But now that we are growing up to our natural resources and find ourselves faced with the problem of learning to live with each other, can we do any better job than the worried peoples of Europe?

Ninety percent of the people of the United States whole-heartedly believe in a higher standard of living, more widely distributed among people who are continually being better educated, who are free to say and do what they please. In spite of all the disillusionments since the World War, we still hold to this dream. But we now know that the understanding and discipline of the average man will have to be more complete than we once thought necessary. The world has changed enormously since the preamble to the Constitution was written. But the spirit of the preamble is just as good today as it was in 1787 and we need this spirit more than ever. But in applying the preamble, we find ourselves faced today with large corporations, labor unions and commercial farmers, whereas in 1787, there were self-supporting plantations, small farmers and shopkeepers.

Some corporations have learned to dodge in and out between the Federal authority and the respective

State authorities and a few have become expert in putting pressure on governors and State legislatures. Leaders of farm and labor organizations have endeavored steadily to checkmate corporations in their use of State and Federal power. The United States has become a battle ground of the pressure groups each of which has profound suspicion of the others. At times it almost seems as though the check and balance system, so dear to the heart of Madison, has succeeded in producing a situation where the preamble to the Constitution should be rewritten in some such terms as:

"We the warring classes of the United States, in order to continue confusion, promote disunity and hard feelings, do hereby declare that each of us will do just as he pleases and that our endeavor shall be to increase our respective profits by doing less work."

This clashing of warring groups often produces results which are against the true realization of the American dream. But this situation may be a necessary preliminary to working out the political and economic system which we really want.

In the America that is to be, I believe that the warring classes can co-operate more consciously for the general welfare than they have in the past. There can be more mutual triumph and less mutual defeat. If to defeat a visible common enemy, we all had to pull together how easy it would be. The buoyant spirit of progressive America would blaze forth, minor differences would be forgotten and our production would increase by leaps and bounds.

The problem of today is whether we can manifest the spirit of unity in the name of the general welfare. Some say that the Constitution of the United States will not permit it. There is no question whatever in my mind that the Constitution does permit this in view of the spirit of the preamble and the debates of those who wrote the Constitution. Unity in the name of the general welfare has all too long been delayed by those who have made the theory of States' rights a refuge for anti-social activities. If the United States is to assume her destiny in the family of nations, there must of necessity be more centralization of certain types of policy making and more decentralization of certain types of administrative responsibility.

In writing a previous book, *New Frontiers*, I became very much aware that any serious thinking about our present national problems inevitably demands still more serious thinking about methods of solution which are in line with our democratic ideals. I suggested that such methods might well be considered under the general head, "The Process of Economic Democracy," and I went so far as to imply that another book with such a title was called for. Certainly I do not offer the present volume as an answer to that self-inflicted proposal, but it does, toward the end, offer some further suggestions.

In explanation of the limited discussion of detailed plans in this book, I can only say that the recent judicial fate of various economic measures of the present administration seems to me to require that we reëxamine the background of our institutions and aims as a nation to find where we stand now, before we draw up detailed plans for moving elsewhere, even though such plans are more than ever needed.

The effort of this book, then, is to take the mind rapidly over some of the high spots in our history so that a sense of motion and direction will appear. If each reader then begins to think of the destiny of America in his own way and if this destiny begins to take form in terms of the long-time general welfare, then the writing of this book will have served its intended purpose.

*　*　*

On reading over this book just before it goes to press, I am aware it may be subject to criticism from a number of points of view. When "prosperity" returns, and most of our unemployed are put back to work as a result of the building boom which is almost certain to develop some time during the next 5 or 10 years, many people will no doubt feel that a book of this sort is unduly alarming. If there is no world catastrophe in the way of war or of weather, it may easily be possible that someone in 1939 might say: "Wallace must have been under the cloud of the depression of the early '30s to have written as he did in 1936."

Writing for the benefit of this possible critic of 1939, I would like to suggest that when the next building boom blows up, as it probably will some time in the '40s, there will ensue a situation which in some respects will be more difficult to meet than the depression of the early '30s, if in the meantime serious efforts to prevent it have not been made. To prepare for such efforts, we need widespread education as to the nature of our governmental and economic history in the light of modern problems. This book, I hope, may help to satisfy this need and be of service to those who wish to prevent or alleviate the depression of the 1940's.

Acknowledgments

I WISH to make acknowledgment here to John R. Fleming, Morris L. Ernst, Philip Glick and Irving Brant for the benefit of discussion with them concerning the Constitution and the Supreme Court and for access to unprinted material collected by Mr. Brant and Mr. Ernst. Ferner Nuhn has been most helpful throughout. Louis Nolan and Carl Taeusch have assisted by the assembly of historical data. Louis H. Bean has checked over the figures having to do with the economic growth of the country.

Doubtless no one of these gentlemen would be in complete accord with everything which is contained in this book, but I nevertheless feel that I owe a debt of gratitude to each of them.

Part One
FORCES OF CHANGE

Chapter I

"A MORE PERFECT UNION": 1787

I F MODERN newspapers had existed in 1787, the news of the time might have been flashed in some such headlines as these:

Angry farmers resist court judgments ... "sound money" advocates unite ... protection against foreign luxury goods demanded ... convention bloc holds only property should vote ... Luther Martin, people's friend, quits convention ... new era of progress seen under Constitution ... Constitution a frame-up, claim ...

The times were crucial. The excitement and high hopes of the War for Independence, successfully waged under the gleaming banner of the Declaration, seemed to be fading away in the cross-purposes and confusion of the peace.

Even Washington, with Valley Forge long behind him, seemed to be bogged in these peacetime morasses. "What astonishing changes a few years are capable of producing," he wrote John Jay. "I am told that even respectable characters speak of a monarchial form of Government without horror.... What a triumph for our enemies to verify their predictions—what a triumph for the advocates of despotism to find that we are incapable of governing ourselves, and that systems founded on the basis of equal liberty are merely ideal and fallacious! Would to God that wise measures may be taken in time to avert the consequences we have but too much reason to apprehend."

In short, the people were finding that the problems of peace are more baffling than the problems of war. With a foreign enemy at the gates, the people will hang together—not wanting to hang separately. Farmers of Massachusetts, planters of Virginia, financiers of Philadelphia, Boston and New York, all had thrown their energies and resources into the common fund. It was far from easy sailing; there were trials and Tories and dissension; but the spirit of unity for the purpose of the war had won out.

After the war, after the serious emergency, it's another matter entirely. People begin to think more shrewdly again of their different interests, the size of their bank accounts, the color of their hair, and the shape of their ancestors' noses! They begin to fall apart.

The loose sort of organization established under the Articles of Confederation, supplemented by committees of correspondence and public safety, and with great reliance placed upon Washington as leader and conciliator of the various factions, had served the purpose of unity sufficiently well during the War for Independence. But after the war, it wasn't long before the Articles were proving too weak and cumbersome to serve the needs of peacetime

unity for four million people in thirteen separate
States stretching a thousand miles from the hills of
New Hampshire to the flats of Georgia.

What was the great war fought for, anyway?

The financiers of Philadelphia, Boston and New
York said: "To make America safe for American capital. And look," they said, "our securities and paper
money are worthless."

The planters of Virginia and the Carolinas said:
"To protect our civil and political rights. And look,"
they said, "we exchanged absolutism for impending
anarchy."

The manufacturers and shippers said: "To promote
our trade and commerce, freed from British commercial restrictions. And look, the people continue
to buy British luxuries."

The small farmers of New England, Pennsylvania,
and the back country of Virginia and the Carolinas
said: "The war was fought to give us common folks
the right to live in freedom, as the Declaration said.
We gave our blood and our lives for that right," they
said. "And look, our creditors are on our backs. The
courts are controlled by the rich people. They send
their militia to take our land away."

Farmers, planters, merchants and financiers all
asked: "Where are our inalienable rights to life,
liberty, and the pursuit of happiness that we were
all shouting for? Unless we do something to insure
those rights, those words were all meaningless."

What did they want to do?

Briefly, there were two general programs. One was proposed by the creditor classes; and that was somehow to strengthen the National Government, give it a strong arm to protect American trade and property rights at home and abroad, begin funding operations for the national debt (which incidentally would make good the securities these people held), and in general establish law and order and safety for money and property in the new nation.

Some of these folks were ready to go to any length to get across this program, even to setting up George Washington or some other reliable character as King of the United States.

The other program was that of the debtors and poor people. It wasn't so much a program as it was an emotion, a blind striking out against oppression. They didn't want the courts to have too much power over contracts and vested rights in property. They didn't care about a sound monetary system; in fact, they wanted cheap money, issued by the States whenever needed, and established in the courts as legal tender. They had thought that the overthrow of the British authority would give them these things, and they had no intention of allowing powerful native interests to take the place of the ousted English interests. So by easy money and contracts, they hoped to pay their debts and get title to their land without too much enrichment of the seaboard capitalists at the expense of their own labor. In effect, they wanted a weak rather than a strong government, localized rather than national power.

Some of these folks, too, were ready to go to considerable lengths to reach their ends. Their agitations had begun before the Revolution, and now, disillusioned of the results of the war, they resumed their rebellious activities with even more passion.

At Exeter, New Hampshire, they had surrounded the meeting house in which the legislature was assembled and threatened the lives of the lawmakers if their demand for an issue of paper currency was refused. They were finally dispersed, but not without the aid of the militia.

In Rhode Island, the votes of the debtor class had won out in the legislature for an issue of new currency. When some people refused to honor the scrip they were upheld by the judiciary. A bitter political feud was precipitated that lasted through the election of the next legislature and resulted in rejection of most of the State's judges, even though the currency ruling remained in force.

In Massachusetts, farmers under the fiery leadership of a man named Daniel Shays (a *desperate debtor*, Hamilton called him) broke up courts in an effort to delay trials against themselves. So great was the sympathy for Shays' movement, so successful was it in impeding debt actions, that Governor Bowdoin felt compelled to send an army against the embattled farmers. The men were dispersed and Shays captured, but sympathy for the movement was so widespread that Shays was not punished; and Governor Bowdoin was defeated in the next election.

These uprisings and pressures were the Farm Holiday movement of that day.

Yes, agrarianism has a long history in our country. Paper money and pitchforks. Inflation or invalidation. Alas, political agrarianism too often hasn't amounted to more than that.

Sometimes the agitation brings notice to the country that farm distress is real, and makes even city people realize that something ought to be done. In other cases, it may act only as a boomerang, bringing results which will plague farmers at a later date. In time agrarians will have to think the thing through, rather than grab at the weapons nearest at hand: money magic or pitchforks. In time they'll have to have a program that gets down to fundamental economic facts, that unites agrarian welfare with the general welfare of the people, and work that program out in the law of the land.

In the 1780's the agrarian debtor agitation alarmed the propertied classes in every State, and greatly strengthened the movement for a strong national government and uniform money and property laws.

It is not an easy matter to decide on the merits of the case as between the warring classes in the 1780's, the small farmers and the privileged moneyed and propertied interests, the "haves" and the "have-nots."

The debtors' and poor people's situation was a hard one. Desirable land had been pretty well monopolized by wealthy landowners and the large land-speculation companies. As yet, there was no genuinely liberal land policy promoted by the Government itself. For some time to come, in fact, the Government was to play into the hands of the large land speculators, because of its pressing need for quick revenue. Not until Jefferson's administration in 1800 was the country to broaden its land program so that it would work out in the interests of the small home-seeker.

Home-seekers in the 1780's had been forced to buy from speculators, often under onerous conditions, or become "squatters" on land they had no title to, with the uncertainties and dangers that entailed. Even George Washington was known to evict a "squatter." Credit from the land companies was on a short time basis, and capital to develop the land had to be obtained from the moneyed people in the older established regions. Between the land speculator and the moneylender, the farmer whose only asset was his own energy had a hard row to hoe. It was a tremendous task to clear virgin land, plant crops, keep alive, and still obtain the cash needed to make payments on debts and contracts. Hence these back-country farmers wanted cheap money and local government that wouldn't enforce contracts too rigidly.

They did, of course—those near the frontiers, at least—want protection from the Indians. But that was about all they wanted from a strong national government.

The Federalists, while some of them were watching out for the interests of the moneyed and propertied classes, certainly held a larger vision of the future of the country. They were aware that, after all, a nation couldn't advance very far with trade on a barter basis, or with a fluctuating and possibly valueless currency. They saw that many of the problems, even in 1787, were national in scope: a sound national credit, a strong enough government to give prestige and safety to its international trade and stable enough internally so that commerce, transportation, and the development of the country's resources might be facilitated. All these things would depend on effective powers of a national government rather than on the haphazard actions of separate States.

It was the Federalists who had a program, who were skilled in political technique, and who pressed for true national action. On February 21st, the Congress of the Confederation called for a convention for the "sole and express purpose" of revising the Articles. Legally, the Convention was not to have gone beyond revision. James Madison, the philosopher of the movement, later challenged the world to deny that the Convention had the right to ignore its instructions and to draw up a totally new instrument of government. "Let them declare," he said, "whether it was of most importance to the happiness of the people of America that the Articles of Confederation should be disregarded and an adequate government be provided and the Union preserved;

or that an adequate government be omitted and the Articles of Confederation preserved."

The Convention met in the early summer of 1787, when the long fight on the issues of the new document began. It might be contended that the Convention was packed by the propertied classes. It is true that few representatives of the debtor and small farmer class were present. Perhaps, in part, that was their fault; perhaps they hadn't been alive to the need and opportunity for threshing out their program in a national forum; perhaps they had seen their problems in too local a light.

Luther Martin of Maryland was one of the few men present who represented and sympathized with the indebted farmers. Speaking on the "obligation of contracts" clause, which was one of the chief bulwarks of property rights written into the Constitution, he made a stirring plea for justice to the indebted classes, especially in times of great scarcity of specie. He said that the times had been when wealthy creditors could practically destroy the poor through their control of money. He warned that such times would arrive again.

Such times *have* arrived, again and again, and perhaps it is unfortunate that Luther Martin lacked support in the Convention for a clause that would have granted emergency powers to lessen the cruel effects of a grinding deflation. Martin disagreed with the final form of the Constitution, and resigned from the Convention.

Yet, when we consider the provisions advocated

by the Federalists which were actually incorporated into the Constitution, the contract clause, the regulation of interstate commerce clause, the provision for levying duties and taxes, the provisions against issuing specie or laying duties by States, we must agree these were on the whole in line with the general welfare.

But we must see that general welfare, in the first place, as it was in the 1780's. Let us do a little traveling about the country to see how the people live, how they work, how they trade, what "the general welfare" is under the conditions of the times.

We shall have considerable trouble going about. We can take sailing vessels along the coasts and into bays and rivers. But on the land we shall have to travel by stage, stopping at inns for the night, taking a couple of weeks or more to go from Boston to Philadelphia. It will cost us about $4.00 to go 45 miles from Baltimore to Georgetown, by land, while we might travel by ship the 300 miles from New London, Connecticut, to Alexandria, Virginia, for only $6.00. When we get off the main roads between the large cities, travel will become even more difficult. We shall have to get about by slowly navigating the rivers in small boats, or by horseback, carrying what we need in saddlebags. Whether by stage or horseback, we shall have to take a ferry at every river of any size, for there are almost no bridges over large rivers. We shall have to pay innumerable tolls, be delayed by bad weather, not always have a clean bed to sleep in, and in general put up with rather primitive conditions.

We might hear about the transportation problem, say in Lancaster, Pennsylvania. There they have iron forges where they produce wheel rims, horseshoes, nails, grills and gratings, and other iron products. Yet the cost of wagon transportation for the 75 miles to Philadelphia is more than twice the amount for shipping the same type of goods all the way across the Atlantic from Liverpool.

This means that Lancaster and Philadelphia virtually do not exist for each other, so far as trade in heavy goods is concerned.

We should learn more about the transportation problem a little later in connection with the Whisky Rebellion, when the farmers of Pennsylvania refused to pay an excise on whisky, because it seemed to them to penalize their trade in corn in the only shape it could profitably be transported to markets. You could put a few gallon jugs of whisky in your saddlebags and carry it to market. You couldn't get a bushel of corn over the trails of Pennsylvania except at a greater cost than the corn was worth.

We will understand still further about the localized nature of exchange of goods, when we sit down to dinner with a family of moderate circumstances in Philadelphia. We have a pork pie made from pork grown four miles away, fed by grain produced on the same farm, with a crust made from wheat flour ground in a mill a mile away, with the grain raised on a farm six miles from town. We get excellent corn bread made from meal ground in a water mill owned by our host's brother-in-law, who lives two miles from town, and gets his corn from neighbors within three miles around him. Butter is made from cream from cows kept by a neighbor only a few blocks away. We have succotash made from sweet corn and beans which our own host raises in his own spacious backyard, the sweet corn being dried and stored for use throughout the year. For dessert, we have an apple cobbler made from apples grown in an orchard just outside Philadelphia. Our host is proud of his grape wine, which he makes himself from grapes grown on the large trellis in his garden. Except for tea, sugar and salt, everything we have eaten comes from within a radius of a few miles.

Our host could not conceive that "the general welfare" could be concerned with regulation of the production or exchange of the products which we have eaten, which have journeyed so short a distance and involved so little handling from field to table.

And our host, who happens to be connected with a recently organized insurance company, is one person out of twenty among the heads of families in this period whose chief means of livelihood is not farming itself. Even most professional men, lawyers, doctors, preachers and teachers, have small or larger farms, from which they obtain most of their food and much of their clothing. For example, if we visited the Reverend Medad Rogers of New Fairfield, Connecticut, we would find this gentleman living on a 100-acre farm and receiving but $100 a year salary to do him for the goods he can't produce himself: household utensils, hardware, paint, molasses, salt, sugar, ginger, tobacco and some kinds of cloth.

Visiting one of the plantations in Virginia, we would of course see a practically complete plant for living, with timber, brick, hides, beef and pork, cotton, flax, fruit, corn, wheat, vegetables, tobacco, all produced on the estate, and to be made into food, shoes, clothes, buildings, liquor, and so on by the millers, shoemakers, spinners and weavers, carpenters, masons, distillers among the slaves of the planter.

Visiting a farm in Massachusetts, we should understand still better why it took 19 persons living on farms in 1787 to produce enough food and fiber above their own needs for one city person and have some left over for export.

The farmer's tools are the plow, the hoe, the sickle, the scythe, the pitchfork. His plow, in 1787, is a cumbersome wooden one. He has a two-wheeled cart for hauling on the farm in summer, and a sled in winter. He fashions the plow yoke and most other wooden parts of his tools himself. The iron parts; chains, axehead, bill hook, hoe blade, and scythe blade are hammered out by the village smith, whom he pays often in wheat, corn or a side of pork.

We watch him plowing in the spring behind his

pair of oxen. We see him sowing by hand, scattering
the seed from a sack, and then covering the seed
with a brush harrow or hoe. When the grain is ripe,
he is in the field with a sickle, back bent, cutting the
stalks, foot by foot across the field, binding and
shocking them by hand. Under the summer sun it is
back-breaking work; sweat rolls down his face and
his heavy homespun shirt soon is wringing wet.

The grain is hauled to the barn in his two-wheeled
cart. There it is threshed with flails or trod out by
oxen. The straw is stacked with a pitchfork.

To produce and harvest one acre of wheat, it has
cost him at least 70 and probably more back-breaking man-hours of labor. And he expects only 10 to 15
bushels of wheat from an acre. Under such circumstances the farmer won't be troubled by surpluses.
The problem is to get enough stuff produced to feed
his own family and have a little left over to sell.

Even so, agricultural exports are important in the
young nation, amounting to perhaps 15 percent of
total domestic production. As early as 1791 the
United States was sending abroad many of the commodities that were to become the mainstays of its
export trade in mature years: 4 million bushels of
wheat including flour, nearly 2 million bushels of
corn, 101 million pounds of tobacco and 6 million
pounds of pork and lard. In addition, the young
nation shipped out some products which later could
not be profitably exported. These included 13 million
pounds of beef and tallow, a million pounds of butter

and cheese, 504,000 bushels of rice and 58 thousand casks of flaxseed.

Our farmer is probably not very progressive in his methods of production and use of land. He doesn't select his seed grain with much care; he doesn't rotate his crops. He found his land very fertile to begin with due to the centuries-old deposit of vege-table matter on the surface, and he doesn't spend much thought and effort keeping it that way. When a farm is "used up" he plans to take up fresh land elsewhere.

As we go about the country, we find it hard to see where farming leaves off and "industry" begins. In fact "industry" in the 1780's means industriousness, and even the word manufacture means "something made by hand." "Commerce" means buying and selling, and has not yet been expanded by Marshall to include navigation and transportation, and then narrowed again by later justices to mean *only* trans-portation so far as the interstate commerce clause is concerned. Clothing, rugs and many other household necessities are made chiefly at home. Shoes and furniture are made largely by village artisans. Spe-cialized "industry" is limited mostly to paper and flour mills, ship-building, some iron and copper works, clocks and watches, hats, some carriage works, and a few other things. One cotton factory, said to be the first in the United States, was set up at Beverly, Massachusetts, in 1787. Power, other than animal and human power, was limited to water power.

Except for the slave labor of the South, a distinct laboring class hardly existed. The small, largely handicraft industries employed apprentices who expected to learn the trade and have shops of their own.

We look in vain for corporate industries in the sense that we know them today. Before 1790, there were but 30 corporations, by 1800 there were over 300, but these were mostly turnpike, bridge, canal or fire companies. Bank and insurance companies numbered 67 by 1800, and there were only 6 incorporated manufacturing companies before the nineteenth century.

Thus, when the Constitution was adopted, "property" meant almost entirely real property; farms, houses, chattels (including slaves) and so forth, and ownership of such property, with 95 percent of the people engaged in agriculture, was widely distributed. It was this type of property that made up the bulk of the property to be protected under the "due process" provision of the fifth amendment. That this provision might apply, some time, to the great holdings of capital, plant and "good will" of the mammoth impersonal corporations of the twentieth century could hardly have been anticipated, nor could it have been anticipated that "due process" would come to mean not merely protection through law, but in many cases virtual immunity from law.

The potentiality of the corporation charter as a privileged instrument under law did not, however, pass unnoticed at the time. In the debates over the granting of a charter to the Bank of North America, one legislator said: "If the legislature may mortgage, or, in other words, charter away portions of either privileges or powers of the State—if they may incorporate bodies for the sole purpose of gain, with the power of making by-laws, and of enjoying emolument of privilege, profit, influence, or power—and cannot disannul their own deed, and restore to the citizens their right to equal protection, power, privilege, and influence—the consequence is that some foolish and wanton assembly may parcel out the commonwealth into little aristocracies, and so overturn the nature of our government without remedy." Thus early was foreseen the dangerous privileges corporations were to obtain from government.

It is true that the commercial classes, under the new Constitution, got the jump on the agriculturalists in obtaining powers from government. Interpreted liberally, the clauses that allowed Congress to lay duties and to regulate foreign and interstate commerce were to become the grounds for a protective tariff. Freedom of capital enterprise to expand indefinitely was to be facilitated by the protection of property rights under various provisions, even by the interstate commerce clause.

In the 1780's, with the exchange of goods narrowly localized, it was inconceivable that agriculture would need powers under government equivalent to the tariff, or the right of business to obtain charters of incorporation. Its welfare seemed assured because of the large amount of land available at relatively low prices and because of its prospects for exports. How much agriculture prospered by the more stable conditions brought about by the new government under the Constitution may be seen from the fact that by 1793 exports—which were almost entirely agricultural—had in three years jumped 44 percent, from $18\frac{1}{4}$ million dollars to 26 million dollars.

Looking back, in spite of our sympathy for the indebted groups, we must agree that small farmers who opposed the Constitution were standing in the way of the building of a nation. Victimized though they were, they were also local in viewpoint, unprogressive, and to a large degree benighted. The group of statesmen in the convention, headed by Madison, won out both against the States' rights extremists on the one side and the monarchial plutocrats on the other.

The problems of the day required "a more perfect union." Extraordinary progress had been made in the past 12 years in the thinking of the American people on the form this union was to take. The Articles of Confederation had envisioned "a Perpetual Union between the States." The preamble of the new Constitution began with words never before used officially in America: "We the people of the United States." The new government was to be a national union of people, and not a union of sovereign and independent States. It was a profound new basis for government.

The preamble voiced the purposes the framers hoped would be accomplished by the new union of people: "establish Justice, insure the domestic Tranquillity, provide for the Common Defence, promote the general Welfare, and secure the Blessings of Liberty to ourselves and our Posterity." In the body itself, the document reiterated the concern of the founders for adequate national power to promote the general welfare in the clause granting powers to the national legislature: "to lay and collect Taxes, Duties, Imposts, and Excises, to pay the Debts and provide for the Common Defence and general Welfare of the United States."

Changes might come with the years, problems might arise which would drastically alter the pattern of what constituted "the general welfare." Yet the instrument of the people in their new union provided that such problems might be dealt with. The Constitution envisioned a true nation, to be controlled by the people, and with powers to deal nationally with national problems.

1597835

Chapter II

FARMERS IN THE SADDLE: 1858

THOUGH farmers were perhaps outmaneuvered by the commercialists led by Hamilton in the early years of the new nation, they had things pretty much their own way most of the time from 1800 to 1858. All through this period the farm population was more than half of the total population. More than anything else, farming people are interested in land. They try to get all they can of it and then they try to sell out at a profit before their debts destroy them. This philosophy was given a broad trial during these years when farmers were in the saddle, with rather sad results.

Both the New England industrial interests and President Jefferson thought the Louisiana Purchase was unconstitutional. Nevertheless the farm desire, the general welfare, and Jefferson's vision of a continental nation justified it. The agricultural interests were in favor of the War of 1812, and the New Englanders helped only grudgingly in the war and some of them openly urged secession as they protested against it. The farmers rode into power in a big way with Andrew Jackson in 1828, and by 1836 and 1837 their land speculation and paper money schemes in the States reached such a pass that the blowup was one of the worst of the nineteenth century. It seems as easy for farmers when they are in power to indulge in weak banking and soft money as it is for financiers to use their control to maintain high interest rates and monopoly.

The Supreme Court justices appointed by Jackson were largely farmer-minded. When the laws having to do with debts, contracts, bankruptcies and similar matters came before them, they tended to take the farm-debtor point of view. Jackson's opposition to Federal banking brought about wild-cat banking in the States and stimulated wild speculation in land. Land speculation always results in a smash, and after the smash there is always a demand for soft money and for debt cancellation. Farmers who are caught in the trap think they benefit from land speculation, soft money and debt repudiation. Actually the whole thing is a nightmare to every one concerned. The United States went through many dark days in this period from the early '30s to the late '50s, during which time the agricultural interests dominated the three branches of the Federal Government of the United States almost without interruption. Farmers of this period were mostly strong believers in States' rights, partly because they thought in this way they could most effectively break down contractual obligations and provide for the issuance of paper money by State banks. Farmers of today cannot be especially proud of the statesmanship of their ancestors during the first half of the nineteenth century. They were greedy, grabbing men, just as were the industrialists who rose to wield great power in the last half of the century, and it is not surprising that more territory was added to the United States from 1800 to 1850 than during all the rest of the history of the country put together.

Gradually during the '40s and '50s, the farmer party which had put Jackson in power in 1828, became split up. Most of it came to represent the slave-owning planters of the South and most of the rest went into Fremont's and Abraham Lincoln's new Republican Party. The slavery issue unfortunately split the northern farmer from his southern brother, a split that was destined to continue almost without interruption for about 70 years.

The rapidity with which the Supreme Court can precipitate an obstinate issue so that the public demands drastic action was never so well illustrated as by the Dred Scott decision in March of 1857. Lincoln criticized the court and in his debates with Douglas made his famous assertion that the nation could not endure half slave and half free. He was beaten by Douglas for the Senate in the election of 1858. The issue which had been so slow in focusing rapidly became the issue of unity. We couldn't live longer half slave and half free. We must become one or the other.

Agriculture, industry and labor before the Civil War were still astonishingly primitive. Even so, the cotton gin, the steel plow and a few other improve-

ments had made it possible for 19 persons living on
farms to provide food and fiber for clothing for
themselves and for 19 persons living in cities instead
of for only one city person as in 1787, and in addition export enough for three persons living abroad.
The binder was coming in slowly but most wheat
was still cut with the cradle. This, however, was an
advance over the sickle of 1787. A primitive threshing machine operated by horses had been invented.
The real improvement in farming would not be felt
until after 1870.

Manufacturing, while still in a relatively simple
stage, had made great headway since 1800, particularly beginning with the Embargo of 1807, and had
become a major source of income in many of the
eastern States. Different sections of the country and
different economic groups were increasingly aware
of their divergent interests, at least from a short-
time point of view. Manufacturers contended for a
land policy that did not make it too easy to secure
public land, since "free land" would tend to draw
labor from the East to the West, and force wages
higher. Wage-earners as well as farmers were anxious
for a liberal land policy, and progressive people such
as Horace Greeley were pointing out that even employers in the East would gain from a more rapid
development of the West, because it would mean
more customers for the products of eastern industry.

Both labor and employers, however, were alarmed
whenever farm prices reached high levels, since this

meant increased cost of living and difficulties between labor and employers in contests over wages.
While no strong labor movement had developed, be-
ginnings had been made as far back as 1827 with
the formation of workingmens' parties in Philadelphia, New York and Massachusetts. The frontier
remained a great reservoir to take up the slack of
unemployment and cushion the shock of hard times.

Just about this time Lord Macaulay was writing
a famous letter to a New York Congressman warning
him that the time would come when the United
States, like her sister nations in Europe, would feel
the confinements of her borders, and then her structure of government would be tested by great depressions, unemployment and the pressures of warring
factions. This time still seemed far away in 1858,
and only an outsider such as Macaulay was de-
tached enough to foresee it. Americans were far too
busy.

Within two years, however, the East and the
West were to make their historic bargain on the
slavery issue, land policy and the tariff, in combination against the South, and within four years the
nation was to be tested in a desperate struggle,
though not of the sort Macaulay anticipated.

The time was one of yeasty ferment. Reformers,
not only against slavery, but land reformers, religious
reformers and economic reformers obtained followers everywhere. Religious and social groups were
establishing colonies on utopian principles, which
flourished for a longer or a shorter period. This fer-

ment had been a stimulus to migration. Sects which found the more densely populated eastern States inhospitable to their beliefs and practices might set out, like the children of Israel, to promised lands in the precarious but tolerant West. The most notable of these migrations was that of the Mormons.

The gold fever that shook the country in 1849 was also a great stimulus to migration. Whether or not the searchers for treasure ever reached the gold fields of California, the lure of gold took thousands of people from the safe, settled regions of the East to adventure and new homes in the West.

The most extraordinary changes have been made in transportation. It is no longer necessary to depend on a navigable river to reach the interior or to travel on horseback. In the '20s and the '30s the Government had laid out a series of national pikes running from New York through Philadelphia and Baltimore to as far west as Indianapolis. The Government's first use of its spending power to promote the domestic welfare was in making it easier for the people of different States to have trade and contact with each other. There was grave debate about the constitutionality of spending Federal money for roads, but the needs of the national welfare finally triumphed. The people realized that a democracy covering so much territory as the United States would have to have its widely separated parts as closely connected as possible by avenues of transportation and communication if it were to think and feel as a unity.

Taverns were built along the pikes; passengers

were carried in Concord coaches; the freight was carried in Conestoga wagons; and the livestock was driven from the West to the great eastern cities on the hoof. The improvements over 1787 brought about by these great Government roads and by semi-public canal enterprises were tremendous. And yet within a very few years, the railroads put the whole system out of business.

Enlightened people saw the railroads as another great unifying force to draw the great, sprawling new democracy together, and the Government opened up its credit and its land resources to help the Empire Builders in their thrilling work. The big period of railroad expansion was to come after 1870, but the new force was already felt by 1858, when thousands of miles of track had been laid. The Empire Builders, however, were not always to work as a unifying force. Their ruthless methods in levying tribute on the communities along their rights of way which they could make or break, their manipulation of stocks, their corruption of legislators, their secret agreements and rebates in favor of privileged customers, were to cause injustices and sectional conflicts for many years to come.

But the farmers were still in the saddle in the first half of the century. During the Jacksonian period they showed that farmers, too, can misuse power, especially with respect to money and banks. During the '40s and especially the '50s the agrarian interests were responsible for another and even more serious misuse of power. The planter-dominated South was in control of the three branches of government, and embittered by the attacks of extreme abolitionists, it used its power to defend and support the institution of slavery in variance with the feeling in the North and in the West where new States were ready to enter the Union.

In the heat of the controversy, the doctrine of unity and the general welfare was lost sight of. The time when farmer domination of the United States was most nearly complete was one of the greatest in physical growth but also one of the greatest in confusion. Even as the confusion of the period of the Articles of Confederation finally resulted in a new sense of national unity, so the confusion of the '30s, '40s and '50s finally precipitated action when the American people declared for and won unity on a new basis, though at a terrible cost.

Chapter III

IN GOLD WE TRUST: 1896

FROM 1858 to 1896 the United States probably made the greatest material advance it ever has made or ever will make in a similar period of time. New territory was not added as it had been during the first half of the century, but existing territory was brought under the plow and tied together by the railroads in a most extraordinary fashion. Business leapt aggressively into the saddle from which the southern planters had been thrown. Inventors were doing amazing and revolutionary things with steam engines and electricity.

Those who happened to get control of railroads, telegraphs, mines, oil and factory systems applied them to the unexploited parts of the world with unprecedented results. Never had capital been mobilized so powerfully before. Never had the world's population increased so fast. Never had there been such an expansion in the production of food and other goods.

The binder and other labor-saving farm machinery, which had no great significance as long as they were used in the Virginia hills, increased the agricultural productivity of an hour of man labor many times on the western prairies and plains.

From 1870 to 1890 agricultural production more than doubled, production of manufactures more than trebled and mineral production more than quintupled.

By 1896, only 45 percent of the people lived on farms instead of the 95 percent which had lived on the land in 1787. The railroad shops, the iron and steel mills, the meat, food, textile, and implement factories needed a larger and larger proportion of the population, while more efficient farming could get along with a smaller proportion.

In 1787, 19 persons on farms could produce enough food above their own needs and for exports for only one city person. In 1858, 19 persons on farms could support 19 city persons. But by 1896, 19 farming people could produce enough food for themselves, for 29 city people and for 5 people abroad.

But if city people were more dependent on farmers in 1896 than they had been in 1787, farmers were also more dependent on city people. No longer do farmers card and spin and weave their own wool and make it into clothes. No longer do they fashion many of their own tools. No longer do they make their own candles and soap.

Instead, they must sell most of their produce to obtain the cash not only for fixed charges and taxes, but for clothes, for expensive machinery, and even for some of their food which it no longer pays them to produce. The farmer, like his fellow citizens in the cities, has become a specialist, and only as he remains a specialist can the people in the cities have enough to eat.

Only about 40 percent of what a farm family in Kansas consumes is produced on the farm. The other 60 percent must be purchased. Three-fourths of the family's income must come from sales, and but one-fourth is made up of things produced and consumed on the farm.

Meanwhile, the farmer's fixed charges have been increasing steadily. As the better land is taken up by settlers, or parcelled out to railroad companies, land values rise; during the '70s they went up by 40 percent. Though some farmers benefit temporarily from the rise, on the whole it means a comparable rise in capital charges. It means greater difficulty for farmers to obtain or retain ownership of their land; in 1880 already one-fourth of all farmers had become tenants, and the percentage increased every decade.

It will be a long time before American farmers think out clearly this land value business. Sometime they will have to decide whether they are primarily real estate operators or producers. During this expanding period, too many of them are thinking of themselves as holders of real estate, with the real money coming from rise in value.

Then, as farming moves westward, the length of the haul for farm produce steadily increases and with it the toll taken by railroads. Farm taxes also continue to rise as settlement thickens over the country.

In short, farmers with other classes were steadily

being drawn into the network of a society based more and more on outlays of capital, on exchange of goods for cash, on widening margins for the handling of goods between the producer and the consumer, and on enlarging industrial units which more and more controlled the conditions under which people worked and the quantities and prices of things people had to buy.

Concentrations of all kinds are going on: concentration of people in cities—now over 30 percent of the population are in cities over 8,000 instead of three percent a hundred years ago—concentration of workers in larger and larger factories, concentration of big enterprises into still bigger and bigger ones, and concentration of capital into the hands of fewer and fewer entrepreneurs and financiers.

These concentrations are having the profoundest effect on people's relations. They are affecting the bargaining power of workers with respect to their jobs; they are increasing the dependence of people producing specialized things on a whole circle of other people who specialize in other things; they are increasing the dependence of every one on the cash wages or profits which will enable him to buy the things he no longer produces himself.

By the end of the nineteenth century, three-fourths of all manufactured products were produced by companies owned by stockholders. Steel, copper, lead, coal, sugar and other necessary products which farmers had to buy in one form or another were getting

into the hands of a few mammoth concerns. Prices
of these products could be pretty well controlled by
the few men at the top.

These men were also rather ruthless in dealing with
labor. One of them, John W. Gates, head of a steel
and wire trust, was suspected of shutting down his
Chicago plant in good times, throwing thousands of
men out of work, simply because he wished to put a
scare into the steel market. Many large employers
brought thousands of workers from Europe under
contract, workers who would accept long hours and
low wages, in order to keep their labor costs at a
minimum. Labor was growing increasingly conscious
of its problems in these changing circumstances.

Thus the lines between warring interests were
drawn on a number of fronts.

Meanwhile, how have those noble concepts of the
preamble to the Constitution been faring in the
hundred odd years since they were phrased? What is
the meaning, in 1896, of Justice, the General Welfare
and the Blessings of Liberty, under the conditions
that have come to pass? What is the state of the
"more perfect Union"?

There have been some important gains. Threats
to the "more perfect Union" by sections or groups
ready to push States' rights to the point of dissolution
of the Union are no longer serious. That battle has
been won, though at the cost of a civil war and many
human lives. In 1896, whatever the conflict of sections or classes, there is little likelihood of any group

getting together, as the slaveocracy had done, and before them a certain group of financiers and manufacturers had done at Hartford in 1814, to threaten dismemberment of the Union if their demands for sectional benefits were not granted.

Other important changes in the interpretation of the Nation's cherished principles, however, have taken place. This is the era, for example, in which the Blessings of Liberty have gradually come to mean something rather different from the ideas of the founding fathers. The founding fathers thought of liberty in terms of personal liberty, liberty of conscience, liberty of religious belief, freedom of speech and press. In the last half of the nineteenth century, liberty began to be thought of by the large employers and moneyed interests as meaning the free initiative of capital to expand as it pleased and the free right of employers to drive such bargains as they could. And their lawyers were convincing the judiciary that liberty under the Constitution did mean these things.

Thus, *life*, *liberty* or *property* as they appear in the due process clause of the fourteenth amendment—put there to protect freed slaves—were being taken over by the corporation lawyers as applying to corporate property. Long ago Justices Marshall and Story had put property rights above legislative power, but it remained for the justices of the last half of the century to interpret the Constitution so as to protect the rights of great corporations to expand freely across State boundaries, gobbling up

the smaller fish in their way, virtually free from regulation by either the States or the National Government.

In 1895, in fact, Justice Fuller ratified the right of
business to occupy a sort of legal no-man's land outside the reach of either State or Federal control, when
he held that the American Sugar Refining Company,
a trust that dominated manufacture and sale of sugar
throughout the country, did not violate the Sherman
Anti-Trust law of 1890.

Obviously States were physically powerless to regulate monopolies to insure fair prices. With the
National Government declared legally powerless, the
trusts were free, under law—or rather under anarchy—to proceed pretty much as they pleased.
Hundreds of combinations of trust size formed in the
next five years.

Thus the business men, after the Civil War, ran
things pretty much their own way. They had the
greatest opportunity they ever had or ever will have
to exploit natural resources. It was a business man's
paradise. Unfortunately, when business men dominate a country, they seem just as likely to make
mistakes as farmers or southern planters. The chief
difference between agricultural exploitation and
business exploitation is that business exploitation is
more rapid and more thorough.

The great challenge to business domination came
in the middle '90s and the great drama of the challenge centered around gold. Gold had been accepted

as a commodity for settling international trade balances by most of the civilized nations. Unfortunately, at the time when both population and the production of goods was expanding most rapidly, gold production began to slow up. During the '70s and '80s especially, the rate of output of goods greatly exceeded the rate of output of gold. Prices over the entire world began to fall during the early '70s and continued to fall through the early '90s. People in the newer parts of the world which had been opened up by the railroads, and especially the farmers, were in debt. When prices fell, they found it impossible to pay the interest on their debts. They said that currency and credit had been contracted and that everything would be made all right if silver could be made a base for currency and credit as well as gold.

Under the gold standard theory, a debtor nation which owes each year $100,000,000 in interest charges must ship out each year $100,000,000 more in goods and services than it brings in. If it fails to do this, then it must either arrange to borrow more money from foreign nations or it must ship out gold or it must default. The farmers, the populists and the silver miners said: "There is one more thing we can do. We can change the rules of the game. We can coin silver as well as gold. If silver is remonetized, prices will start rising and farmers will no longer suffer from such unjust debts. Labor will be re-employed, and the world will be happy again."

Weather was bad in the early '90s and especially
in 1894. Exports from the United States were greatly
reduced and for several years we found it necessary
to ship out $50,000,000 of gold annually. Prices were
low, credit was scarce and many laboring men were
out of work. It was a world-wide phenomenon, although somewhat worse in the United States than
most other places, because we had over-expanded
more and because the bad weather of 1894 had hit us
harder, therefore making it necessary for us to lose an
uncomfortably large proportion of our scanty gold
stocks. President Cleveland found himself in the
uneasy position of being dependent on an American
banking house with strong British connections.

Unrest, in this trying time, had shown itself in the
bloody Homestead strike, the Pullman strike, the
march of Coxey's army. The nation was beginning to
realize that the problems of democracy under industrialization, with large consolidations of capital and
the means of production on the one hand and masses
of almost propertyless workers on the other were quite
different from those of a democracy of freeholders of
land as dreamed of by the founding fathers.

Both laborers and farmers, in the latter half of the
century, had been organizing in an effort to meet the
problems they were faced with under the new
conditions.

Labor tried various forms of organization; under
the National Labor Union, the Knights of Labor and
then the American Federation of Labor. Hampered

by the violence of anarchistic fringes in its own ranks, by the weapon of the injunction used against it in the courts, and by a hostile public opinion often misled by a hostile press, labor was moving on its long road toward the right to meet a collective industry by collective bargaining on its own part.

Farmers had made considerable progress since the time of Shays' Rebellion in thinking through their problems and in organizing for effective action. The Grange had demonstrated what an enlightened farm organization could accomplish. Largely through its efforts the Interstate Commerce Act of 1887 had been passed which in time was to allow regulation in the public interest of railroad rates and prohibition of rebates and other discriminatory practices.

Through the agitation of farm organizations, the National Government was taking increasing interest in agriculture. The Department of Agriculture had become a full-fledged executive department in 1889. The Department, it is true, viewed the welfare of agriculture largely in terms of gathering of statistics and of testing seeds and plants. Economic factors did not concern it. In fact, the Secretary of Agriculture in 1895, in a year when cotton sold for around 7 cents, wheat for 60 cents, and corn for 20 cents, prepared a paper to show that there could be no depression for agriculture when farmers were producing enough to feed themselves, feed city people and produce 61 percent of the exports.

The Grange and other organizations, such as the

National Farmers' Alliance and the Southern Alliance, began to feel their way toward such programs as co-operative marketing and storage loans. In 1889, there was a tentative approach between farmers' organizations and labor organizations on the proposal of government ownership and operation of railroads.

The farm depression of the '90s, however, widened the revolt in the agricultural regions. The People's Party formed in 1890, and such battle-cries were heard as that of Mary E. Lease, of Kansas, who urged farmers "to raise less corn and more hell." "We were told two years ago," Mrs. Lease cried, "to go to work and raise a big crop and that was all we needed. We went to work and plowed and planted; the rains fell, the sun shone, nature smiled, and we raised the big crop they told us to; and what came of it. Eight-cent corn, ten-cent oats, two-cent beef, and no price at all for butter and eggs—that's what came of it."

Much in this spirit, thirteen hundred delegates met at Omaha on July 4, 1892, and established the Populist Party. On the platform of a legal tender currency, silver coinage at 16 to 1, a graduated income tax, government operation and ownership of the railroads, the telephone and the telegraph, they secured a million votes in the election. These votes of protest were indication that, even in the expansive '90s, rugged individualism had not brought uniform riches and comfort to free Americans.

During the next four years, the flames fanned by

Cleveland's forcing a repeal of the Sherman Silver Purchase Act and by the Supreme Court's 5 to 4 decision declaring the national income tax law unconstitutional, the revolt spread still further.

This was the background for the battle of 1896. When the Republicans under the tutelage of Mark Hanna nominated the docile and conservative McKinley, and the Democrats, their right wing submerged beneath left-wing enthusiasm and eloquence, nominated Bryan as the frank spokesman of the lowly—the wage laborer, the country lawyer, the crossroads merchant, the farmer and the miner—it looked as if for the first time in decades the lines were clearly drawn between privilege and underprivilege in a national struggle.

McKinley's platform held high the gold standard. The Democratic platform endorsed free silver, repudiated the injunction and demanded jury trial in labor disputes, and criticized in vigorous language the Supreme Court for its income tax decision, which was to cause a delay of nearly two decades in making the income tax legal through a constitutional amendment. The campaign was torrid and dirty. Mammoth torchlight processions lit the sky from coast to coast; speakers donned shining armor from which they hurled muddy epithets. Bryan was called a puppet of "Altgelt the anarchist and Debs the revolutionary" and his campaign one against the Ten Commandments. McKinley was called a chore-boy for the trusts and an exponent of "corporate rapacity" and "the divinity of pelf."

Dispassionately viewed, the division seemed clear.
Labor and the farmers of the South and West would
apparently have everything to gain from reforms in
the use of the injunction and in taxation on the principle of ability to pay and in a liberalization of the
currency. Henry and Charles Francis Adams, life-
long Republicans, scholars and aristocrats of Federalist ancestry, agreed that justice at this time was on
the side of the silverites who wanted to break the
money monopoly under gold. All these reforms, in
one way or another, would be brought about in time.

Why was it that the ranks of farmers and labor
were divided when the election came? How was it
that these large groups, who made up the majority
of the nation, voted against their own interests in
sufficient degree to turn the tide and postpone for
years the desirable reforms?

We must pay tribute to the astuteness of the king-
maker, Mark Hanna, who directed the Republican
campaign. His candidate was bound to him by a large
personal debt of some years standing. His quiet and
largely undercover rallying of big business was effective. Some 4 million dollars is reported to have
passed through Hanna's hands, and over a hundred
million campaign pamphlets were issued from the
Chicago headquarters. James J. Hill, silently shifting
parties, bought a newspaper in St. Paul to see that
the people had a proper angle on the issues. Workers
everywhere were assured by their employers that
victory for Bryan would paralyze industry and lose

workmen their jobs. Mark Hanna was teaching big business how an election campaign should really be run.

No doubt thousands of workers and farmers were sincerely convinced by the "sound money" cry. Yet there were more deepseated influences which split agrarian and labor forces where otherwise they would have been united.

Chief of these influences was the severance of the agricultural South and the agricultural West, stemming from the Civil War, and based on issues which no longer counted but which still held their emotional charge. The West and the Northeast, in the great amalgamation at Chicago in 1860, had joined forces on a combination free soil, high tariff and "vote-yourself-a-farm" platform. The West had been willing to stand for the East's high tariff, providing the East stood for a liberal homestead policy. But by 1896, free soil was a dead issue, free land was of diminished importance, because the better lands had already been settled, and high tariff remained of benefit chiefly to the industrial East and actually penalized the agricultural West.

Western farmers now had the opportunity to heal their breach with their Southern brothers and join in a program that would bring a better balance between agriculture and the consolidating forces of industry.

Too few Western farmers, however, had thought through the problems of the day to cast themselves loose from their historic political moorings. Mark Hanna and the tacticians of the Republican Party were able to use the old bargains and the old prejudices as a wedge to keep the agrarian West and the agrarian South apart. Free trade and free silver were painted as disloyal to the Grand Old Party which had given political birth to the West. The pressures and scares of the campaign won out; many progressive and agrarian leaders, who later became Bull Moosers, were to be ashamed of the part they played in sanctifying gold and monopoly in 1896. Except for the far western States, only Nebraska, Bryan's State, left the fold and voted with the South; the rest of the Middle West went along with the solid East.

Thus the progress toward meeting nationally some of the problems which had become national in scope due to revolutionary economic changes was postponed for the time being. Big business, with its benefits and abuses, was to have free rein under a government that paved the way for centralization of industry, but had no means of centralizing governmental action for other groups on a similar scale.

Looking back, we can see that the issue of gold versus silver was not so important in itself. It was only part of the larger issue of big business welfare versus the welfare of the people as a whole. Actually, it would not have made a great deal of difference whether the gold bugs or the silver bugs won out in 1896. As it happened, world gold production began once more to advance in the '90s and eased the currency situation before Bryan and his farmers realized it.

And in 1896, there were still a number of cushions which fortunately could absorb the shocks of periodic depressions, deepening though they were because of increased industrialization. One was exports. As long as the United States remained a debtor nation, the high tariff would not prevent large farm exports from being sent abroad, which would act as a safety valve for business and agriculture at home. The second was the frontier. In spite of the receding public domain, there were still large areas of arable farm land which could be profitably homesteaded, and which would serve to lessen farm distress and take up the slack of unemployment in hard times.

By good fortune, the United States was still protected from its own mistakes in 1896. The "more perfect Union" under gold and the great corporations forged ahead. But in time it would come face to face with its underlying problems, and there would be no cushions to save it from shock.

Chapter IV

DOWN TO THE SEA IN SHIPS: 1919

UNITED belief and action are easy for a nation riding high on the crest of patriotism, high prices, hungry foreign customers, and a newly awakened sense of power in world affairs. The United States in 1917, 1918 and 1919 was like a young giant, just come of age, and not knowing its own strength. It showed the mixed impulses of youth in its inexperienced idealism, its vaulting ambition, its changeableness, its tendency toward quick disillusion.

The tragedy of 1919 for the United States lay in its failure to understand the basis of its new position. The foundation of its new strength and prosperity was international, yet it refused to accept responsibility for this fact. Its thinking was muddled. Either a nation should keep to itself, paying the price of isolation, or it should be willing to follow up its entrance in world affairs and pay the price of world responsibility. The United States tried to secure the advantages of both positions without accepting the responsibilities of either. As a result, it was to pile up grief for itself both abroad and at home.

President Wilson found himself caught between the two fires. More than any other man, he knew the kind of responsibility the nation under his leadership had let itself in for. He had helped take down barriers on the road to participation in international affairs. Down this road had passed a procession of goods, followed by credit, followed by marching men and more goods and more credit. Wilson, having taken the road, was willing to face the prospect at the road's end. But the nation, because it had never really prepared itself by mature thought for the road it had traveled, and because it quickly became disillusioned of the spiritual things it expected to accomplish, turned its back on its new venture and new responsibility. President Wilson, outsmarted abroad and rebuffed at home, was virtually isolated. The country hankered for its youthful irresponsibility, which it thought of as "normalcy." But "normalcy" such as the country wanted was a dream and a delusion. The nation had yielded up its innocence, and would have to pay the price in one way or another. It was an adult nation, whether it wanted to be or not.

In all truth, the transition had been bewilderingly abrupt. The nation had gradually been approaching maturity up to 1914. Its period of internal expansion had gradually been drawing to a close; the frontier and free lands were becoming a thing of the past. Yet, up to 1914, it still owed large sums of money abroad, and its psychology was that of a youthful nation undergoing rapid development, dependent on foreign money and on a balance of exports over imports for its advancement.

Then, in a few feverish years, it was catapulted
to economic maturity. Abruptly the nation crossed
the dividing line, and from being a net debtor, became a net creditor in the family of nations. Internally, profitable expansion into the remaining areas
of uncultivated land was at an end, or nearly so.
Physically and financially, the country was grown
up. Unfortunately, its psychology did not keep pace
with the change in its economic status. It still acted,
and for some time would continue to act, like an
economic adolescent.

The rate at which the country had been advancing
industrially confused the nation with respect to its
new position. A country in which infant industries
were springing up and expanding with such great
velocity found it difficult to think in terms of financial maturity. Electric power, which had barely been
tapped in 1896, and which in 1904 was used to the
extent of less than 5 billion kilowatts, reached a consumption of almost 40 billion kilowatts in 1919.
In 1896, only 16 motor vehicles were registered in the
country; by 1919, automobile factories had put over
$7\frac{1}{2}$ million automobiles and trucks in operation over
the nation's highways. These new and growing industries tended to encourage the country in its
booming adolescent psychology.

Concentration and consolidation had proceeded
apace. At the end of the nineteenth century, 66 percent of all wage earners were hired by incorporated
companies. By 1919, almost 87 percent of the wage

earners worked for corporations. Now over 43 percent of the population live in cities of over 8,000, as
compared with 33 percent in 1900, and only 3 percent in 1790.

The nation had made some efforts at dealing with
the problems of increasing concentration. Theodore Roosevelt had shaken his big stick at the trusts;
President Wilson had submitted his "five brother"
bills designed to regulate finance and commerce.
The Federal Trade Commission was set up and the
Clayton Anti-Trust Act was passed. Delayed for 18
years by the reactionary 5–4 decision of the Supreme
Court in 1895, the income tax finally became law
in 1913, with ratification of the sixteenth amendment. The Federal Reserve Act had been a step
forward in banking. But the war had put an end to
this movement, and after the war, the big corporations were to continue expanding at an accelerated
pace, finding means to avoid such restraints as had
been put upon them.

Improvements in farming efficiency have made
possible the continued shift of the population from
country to town. In the great wheat regions, the
combine has come into general use, and farmers are
beginning to turn from animal to tractor power.
An acre of wheat in the Great Plains region can be
produced by modern machinery with 3 or 4 hours of
man labor.

Now 19 persons living on farms produce food and
clothing material for 44 persons in cities and for 15

people living in war-devastated countries abroad—a
fact which would have seemed incredible to the
farmers of 1787.

The Federal Government is doing everything
possible to expand agricultural production. New
homestead acts in 1911 and 1916 were more generous
than ever in giving away the remaining public
domain. Grazing is allowed on Government-owned
land with little or no regulation. Through 1919, 125
million dollars has been spent to bring desert lands
into production through irrigation projects.

With the war, the Government's efforts to stimulate agriculture were greatly speeded up. Between
1914 and 1919, county agents and Extension Service
workers were increased from 1,400 to 6,000, and the
annual expenditure was boosted from $1\frac{1}{2}$ million
dollars to $14\frac{1}{2}$ million dollars. Agricultural planners
gathered to map a campaign for intensifying food
production. Congress passed one act after another—
the Food Production Act (to "provide further for the
national security and defense by stimulating agriculture"), the Food Administration Act, the Garden
Commission Act—to help speed up food production.

Councils of Defense sprang up in the States to
help farmers obtain seeds, tractors, and other things
necessary to stimulate production. Gardens trebled
in area. In place of petunias and gladiolas, the
potato plant became fashionable in the gardens of
socialites, almost as if a Potato Act had been passed.

"Food will win the war!...A hog is worth a

shell!" were dinned in farmers' ears, while meatless Mondays and the virtues of oleomargarine and graham flour were urged upon patriotic housewives.

Farmers plowed up permanent pasture and planted corn; they turned over the native buffalo and grama grass of the semi-arid plains regions from western Texas to the Dakotas and planted wheat.

Altogether, 50 million acres of pasture, range, or forest land came into cultivation to meet the demands created by the war and to further the expansion policy of the Government. No one questioned the legality of the Government spending to influence local agricultural production in the direction of expansion.

Factory production was speeded up under the War Finance Corporation's stimulation; $2\frac{1}{2}$ million workers were added to industry. Almost 2 billion dollars of the Government's money was advanced to create a shipping fleet. Down to the sea in ships, along with American soldiers, went the products of an American agriculture and industry thrown into high gear. Rising through 1917 and 1918, farm shipments reached an all-time peak in the crop year ending June 30, 1919. In twelve months, the country sent abroad 287 million bushels of wheat, $5\frac{1}{2}$ million bales of cotton, almost 3 billion pounds of pork and lard, 600 million pounds of beef, and 34 million pounds of butter. Except for cotton, these exports averaged about three times the usual level of exports before the war.

An increase of 50 million acres in land under cultivation, a step-up around 200 percent in many of our major exports: these were measures of the Government's success in expanding agriculture "to provide for the national security and defense."

Certain ominous signs were not lacking. Farm land felt the stimulus of eager investment and speculation funds from all sources, both rural and city. By 1919, land values had almost doubled over those of 1910. A few voices were raised—in a whisper, at least—to suggest that the best agricultural land in the world wasn't worth $300 or $400 as an actual investment, and would be ruinous to the farmer who was forced to work it at that level of capitalization. A few people shook their heads over the increase in the farm mortgage debt, which had risen from $3\frac{1}{3}$ billion in 1910 to almost 8 billion, as of 1920. As editor of a farm paper I urged that this was the time to pay off farm debts, and that they ought to be paid off promptly.

Almost no one was questioning whether the tremendous expansion and intensification of agriculture was in line with good land use. The American farmer had never been a model of thriftiness in the conservation of his soil. Having skinned off one farm, he could too easily move on to virgin land, with its accumulated humus and fertility, and start the skinning process over again. It is true that movements had been started early in the twentieth century which took a longer view of the land in relation to national welfare. Under Theodore Roosevelt, the Government began the notable practice of reserving areas of the public domain, particularly forest and scenic areas, from private entry and exploitation. Inspired by Gifford Pinchot and Horace Plunkett, the Country Life movement had got underway, and Roosevelt appointed a commission in 1908 to further the movement. The group was one of the few public groups interested in conservation.

The feverish expansion of the war period had encouraged the American farmer in his tendency to mine his soil for all it was worth. The program of expansion blindly ignored what might happen to the top soil of millions of acres of dry range land brought under the plow for wheat, and the millions of acres of hillside pasture that had been plowed up and seeded to grow crops such as corn and cotton.

The country was savoring its war boom prosperity in 1919, and was not thinking of after effects. Prices reached incredible heights; wages of labor were increased and hours reduced to a degree never effected before; businesses and corporations, which had learned how pleasantly paternalistic the Government could be in war time under the guidance of their own dollar-a-year men, were counting huge profits and building up great corporate surpluses. Credit continued to be easy on the basis of the huge war debt.

The nation did not consider the foundation of its prosperity under the new conditions. Europe was sending large orders for goods needed to reconstruct

its war-damaged economy. How was Europe to
continue to pay for these orders which were turning
the wheels of American industry and stimulating
American agriculture so vigorously? In 1914 the
United States had owed foreign nations a net amount
around 3 billion dollars. Within a few years, the
balance was on the other side of the ledger, and by
1922, foreign nations were to owe the United States
a net sum amounting to 16 billion dollars. How was
the United States to continue sending abroad the
1917–1921 annual average of around 3 billion dollars
worth of farm products and 3 billion dollars worth
of other products when foreign nations owed us
16 billion dollars and when we wished to take very
little goods from them in exchange? If Europe
couldn't continue to buy our farm products under
these conditions, or if she went back to producing
more of her own food, what was to happen to the
American agricultural plant which was expanded by
50 million acres? These acres couldn't be retired as
easily as were the extra factory workers who were
about to be thrown out of jobs in 1921.

President Wilson was almost alone in 1919 in
having considered the significance of the nation's
new position. In his message to the sixty-sixth Congress on December 2nd, he pointed out the fundamental change that had taken place in America's
relation to world affairs and said, "Anything which
would tend to prevent foreign countries from settling
for our exports by shipments of goods into this

country could only have the effect of preventing them from paying for our exports and therefore of preventing the exports from being made. . . . If we want to sell, we must be prepared to buy. Whatever, therefore, may have been our views during the period of growth of American business concerning tariff legislation, we must now adjust our own economic life to a changed condition growing out of the fact that American business is full grown and that America is the greatest capitalist in the world."

The American nation refused to face the facts as Wilson realistically presented them. The United States was indeed full grown and the greatest capitalist in the world, but in 1919 and for many years afterward she was to act like an irresponsible child.

Her traditional leaders refused to meet the new challenge. Farmers thought they could go on indefinitely keeping under cultivation the extra 50 million acres they had plowed up and continue to expect $2 wheat and $200 land. Labor was preparing to insist that wages be kept indefinitely at twice the prewar level. The great corporations were preparing for an unprecedented era of expansion, pyramided holdings and pyramided stock values. International bankers in Wall Street, while warned by some of their economists in words not greatly different from Woodrow Wilson's, were preparing to subsidize the new prosperity on the shaky basis of the investment of billions of dollars of American peoples' money in credits to foreigners which could not reasonably be paid back. The politicians, realizing the disillusionment of Americans with their European war experience, were preparing to cater to expediency by raising tariffs.

For the moment, the country could remain united on the wave of patriotism, high prices, and huge cargoes sent down to the sea in ships. But the seeds were being sown for the most profound disunity and disillusion. Woodrow Wilson, in his analysis of our creditor position, was a voice crying in the wilderness. Before the American people would be willing to consider his advice they would have to go through an adventure in pseudonormalcy, an adventure in the flotation of foreign loans, an adventure in slapping good customers' faces by higher and higher tariffs and at the same time expecting greater exports, an adventure in Wall Street's bull market, and the experience of the most profound smash in American history. The American people did not know it, but the war was not over in 1919; it had hardly begun.

Chapter V

STEWING IN OUR OWN JUICES: 1932

THE tale of what happens after an important war had been told a thousand times throughout history, and it was always the same tale. The merchants of Athens knew the story; the traders of Rome knew it again and again; the peasants of France and the farmers of England knew it to their sorrow. Prices of wool and olives and grain that had kited sky high dropping with a sickening crash; inflated debts having to be paid off in expensive money; bull traders routed by bears; sheriff's sales and bankruptcies. History had grown weary repeating this trite tale.

Yet, after 1918, the tale seemed to lag. History appeared to have gone back on itself. True, in 1921, farm prices dropped and business slackened, and for a time it seemed as if the story were coming true. But business quickly recovered and agriculture partly recovered. The years went by: 1924, and all seemed firm again; 1926, and a new surge was felt, stronger than ever; 1928, and the lid was off. People became convinced that what happens after wars was an old wives' tale, as out of date as the candle snuffer or hoop skirts. In the 1920's, the world was different.

Then came 1929, then 1930, 1931 and 1932.
Business statisticians had to buy new charts, with
extra-deep sections at the bottom. History, apparently, had only been holding back. The tale had come
true after all, and the climax was all the more
devastating for being delayed.

If the country had gone down to the sea in ships in
1919, it was definitely back home again by 1932,
and stewing in its own juices.

The $3\frac{1}{2}$ billion dollars worth of farm stuff sent
abroad in 1918–1919 had shrunk to a half a billion
dollars. Cotton, at a ruinous 6 cents a pound, was
still finding a foreign market, but wheat exports had
dropped from almost 300 million bushels to less than
50 million; pork and lard exports had dropped from
nearly 3 billion pounds to 700 million pounds.

The stuff we could no longer ship abroad had been
piling up in granaries, warehouses, and on the farm:
almost 13 million bales of cotton, and nearly 400
million bushels of wheat. Surpluses were three times
the usual amount. Farmers, with the continued
advice and encouragement of the Government, had
been producing with increased efficiency for this
disappearing foreign market. With no means of
adjusting output, farm production clogged up the
domestic channels and well nigh suffocated the
country.

Industry as much as agriculture was stewing in its
own juices in 1932. But with the means at hand to
reduce production and an established policy of

doing so whenever necessary, the surpluses of industry took the form of unused resources, unused machinery and capital, unused labor. Probably some 15 million people were out of jobs by the end of February, 1933. These unemployed people, with their productive capacity cut off and their income and purchasing power unavailable, were the contribution of the capitalistic system of industry and business to the stagnated surpluses of 1932 and early 1933.

Through most of the 1920's, the country as a whole saw few portents of the reckoning that would have to be made in the early '30s. Economic processes were accelerating tremendously. Consumption of electric power per person more than doubled between 1919 and 1929. Production of petroleum nearly trebled.

The big corporations were coming more and more to dominate the business and industry of the country. In 1919, the 200 largest industrial, utility, and railroad corporations owned assets worth 44 billion dollars. This was an increase of 68 percent over the assets of the 200 largest corporations in 1909. But by the end of 1929, their assets had increased 85 percent more and reached 81 billion dollars, or half the entire corporate wealth of the country. From 1922 to 1928, these big corporations were growing at a rate more than three times as great as the rate the national wealth as a whole was increasing. If they should continue to expand at the present rate, they

would control 70 percent of corporate wealth by
1950.

A new issue was shaping up, comparable to the
issue that divided the country in 1858. Can the
nation exist half corporate and half "free"? The
corporate part of the nation's economic life was
becoming more and more intrenched through its
power to build up surpluses and to command the
powers of mass production to affect the volume and
prices of the things produced, to influence State
governments, to control parties and to mold public
opinion. Able to hire the shrewdest legal talent
available, it was becoming more and more intrenched
in its rights under law. On the other hand, the small
retailers, the farmers, and other groups whose
business was less susceptible to incorporation, and
who lacked the resources to build up surpluses and
to hire the best legal talent, were more and more at
a disadvantage. In a crisis, they would fall like
ninepins, while the big corporations would survive.

The crisis, however, was still ahead through most
of the '20s. Improved farming efficiency, while it did
not result in much greater income to farmers, was
enabling industry's expansion to take place.

During the 1920's, 6 million people migrated from
the farms of the country to the cities to enter factories, businesses and the professions. The $6\frac{1}{2}$ million
farm families who continued to work the country's
farms could readily supply the rest of the country's
food and fiber, and produce more than enough for
export.

The attention of the country in the '20s however, was centered on business and finance. As the market value of the stocks on the New York exchange mounted from 27 billion dollars in 1925 to 67 billion at the beginning of 1929, the New Era was proclaimed. Much of the country believed that, with finance capitalism given its head, the whole nation would be swept to higher and higher levels of prosperity. A popular weekly pictured an airplane in an endurance flight refueling in mid-air, and made fun of the old fashioned economist down below who was saying it couldn't be done. The economic aeroplane was to keep on gaining elevation indefinitely, with the millennium just around a cloud.

What was the basis for this super-optimism? Why, ten years after the war, could the nation continue to disregard the usual facts of postwar deflation?

The cartoon published by the popular weekly was a better illustration of the actual situation than almost any one would have realized at the time.

That refueling of the American economic ship was being accomplished with money which the United States was continually lending to Europe, so that Europe could continue to buy the products we had to keep selling her, if we were to keep our expanded agriculture and industry going full tilt and thus maintain the capital and price structure at home on the postwar level.

That was the fact which obscured for the time being the actual situation of the United States following the war. That was the fact which post-poned history's tale of what happens after wars.

From being a net debtor to the extent of 3 billion dollars in 1914, the country had become a net creditor to the extent of 16 billion dollars in 1922, and by the end of 1929, to nearly 19 billion dollars.

There were roughly four theoretical possibilities for meeting this change in our financial relationship with the rest of the world.

First, we might have reduced our tariffs to the point where European nations could have shipped into the United States enough stuff to pay interest and principal on their debts and also pay for the cotton, wheat and other products we wanted to ship them. We didn't choose this method. Instead, we raised our tariffs, once in 1922, again in 1930.

Second, we could have kept our tariffs at a high point and still shipped goods abroad, providing foreign nations could pay for them and also pay their debts in gold. Foreign nations tried to do this. They shipped gold to the United States in such quantities that our gold stocks increased from $2\frac{3}{4}$ billion dollars in 1919 to 4 billion dollars in 1929. But there wasn't enough gold in the world to meet the situation in this manner.

Third, we could have decided to forego our export trade in large part, and adjust our economy at home to an internal balance. Forceful reasons might have been advanced for such a course, reasons concerned with a desirable balance between funds needed for

capital investment and funds needed to sustain
purchasing power; with a desirable balance between
agriculture and industry; with a desirable balance
between the fertility taken out and the fertility put
back into the soil. We didn't choose this method.
On the contrary, we continued to mine our soil for a
disappearing foreign market and to pile up capital
beyond the needs of investment until 15 billions were
immobilized in sterile speculation, corporate surpluses or other unusable savings.

One course remained, and this was the course we
followed—until it became an absurdity. We could
keep on lending Europe the money she needed to
pay interest on the debts she owed us and to buy the
products we wanted to sell her. This was the international refueling device that for 12 years kept our
economic aeroplane above the towering peaks of our
credit structure and the massive wall of our tariff,
in Cloud-Cuckoo Land.

When it finally became apparent that subsidizing
the world to pay interest on our own money and to
pay for our own exports was an Alice-in-Wonderland
way of doing business, the loans ceased. Meanwhile
the top-heavy market structure, founded on un-
realities as it was, toppled and crashed. The great
refueling-stratosphere-prosperity flight was over. We
were back to earth, stewing in our own juices.

Stewing in our own juices in 1932, we began to see
that of the four theoretical possibilities for adjusting
the nation to its changed credit position after the

war, only two were actually practicable. Either we could lower tariffs and take in more goods to pay for our exports and for debts owed us, or we could adjust our internal economy on a stay-at-home basis. America's choice had to be one or the other, or some planned middle road between the two. But by 1932, no progress had been made in either direction.

The whole problem, in fact, had become immensely more difficult because for 12 long years the country had been working in opposite directions from either of these policies.

The tariff, as we have noted, was stepped up in 1922, and again by the incredible Smoot-Hawley Act, in 1930. One of the leading financial writers of New York City had come down to Washington when the 1922 tariff act was pending and had brought to the attention of those high in Government reasons why the tariff should be lowered rather than raised. If the tariff were not lowered, he said, the opportunities offered by our creditor position for increasing our wealth by imports would not only be lost, but new troubles would ensue. Those who heard him questioned the political feasibility of his advice.

Again in 1927, the wisdom of indefinitely financing our exports by loaning money was questioned, but the answer was made that not until the United States loaned abroad as much as 40 billion dollars would there be cause for concern. Only one who is thoroughly acquainted with Washington political routine can understand how readily expediency replaces judgment in matters of fundamental long-time policy.

It is true that loans to Europe kept our exports from dropping off almost immediately after the war, instead of after 1930, when loans ceased. But when Europe stopped payment on debts owed us, it became apparent that our exports during the 1920's had largely been given away. We had shipped billions of dollars' worth of our soil fertility to Europe —and Europe paid us back with our own money! It was one of the most prodigal gifts in history.

Our own barriers put in the way of foreign trade were reinforced by the barriers other nations were raising. Beginning about 1925, European nations, fearing future wars, became anxious to be as self-sufficient as possible. Those with an unfavorable balance of trade or with debts to pay off tried to balance their books by restricting imports and stimulating exports. The result was an international rash of tariff-raising, import quotas, domestic subsidies, private agreements and the like, all of which made exchange more and more difficult.

As the export road to solution of our own problem became less practicable, the need for internal adjustment became more pressing. Logically, everything possible should have been done at home to lessen the shock of our becoming a creditor nation.

But our policy took the opposite direction here, too. Agricultural policy continued to be one of stimulation, even though large exports were no longer in line with the general welfare. The personnel of the Extension Service of the Department of Agriculture had been kept on the expanded basis of 1919, and its activities had steadily increased. The Land Grant Colleges and the Experiment Stations were providing more and more information on efficient farming, and farmers, anxious to cut their costs below falling prices were in the mood to listen. With market demands kept in mind, increased efficiency in farming, of course, would have been all to the good. Normally it should mean lowered costs and better income to farmers, with no increase in price to consumers. But in view of a high tariff policy, reduced foreign markets, and an expanded agricultural plant, it was only one more fact to add to the irony of distress in the midst of abundance.

Because of its vulnerable export position, agriculture in 1921 had already felt the shock of the aftermath of the war, when farm prices within two years were cut nearly in half and thousands of farmers lost their farms. Agriculture partly recovered from this first postwar depression, largely because our lending policy artificially sustained exports. But it did not share in the boom period that followed to any great extent. During the height of the boom years, from 1926 through 1929, farm bankruptcies averaged more than 6,000 a year, or six times the normal rate. The farm mortgage debt, which had been $3\frac{1}{3}$ billion in 1910, increased during the 1920's from less than 8 billion dollars to more than 9 billion.

Beginning in 1922, farmers and farm organizations began their long fight for Government recognition of the farm problem and a national farm program that would deal with the situation the Government had helped bring about at the time of the war. In this long fight, farmers educated themselves in the realities of our highly integrated economic system as they had never done in any previous period. The majority of them had come to see that fooling with the currency, while it might lessen the load of debts and taxes, would not in itself bring about a magical solution to the problem of low prices for the things they had to sell and high prices for the things they had to buy. More and more they were seeing the relation of their problems to the tariff and international trade and to the relative advantage of collective action on the part of large industrial organizations as against the individual action of 6 million farmers.

I have told elsewhere the story of that long twelve-year fight which again and again was carried through the legislative body of the National Government, only to be rebuffed by an administration which favored greater protection for industry under the tariff and broader collective action for corporations, but refused agriculture any equivalent powers under government. Farmers, according to the philosophy of the party in power, were to cherish the rugged individualism which long ago had been resigned by business.

Rugged individualism for farmers in 1932 meant 6-cent cotton, 10-cent corn, 2-dollar hogs and 30-cent wheat. For small business men it meant a losing fight against the chain stores and the corporations which, with their built-up reserves, could survive the depression. For the 15 million unemployed heads of families and unemployed young people it meant the liberty of taking the road to look for non-existent jobs, the liberty of holding out the hat for private or local charity, the liberty to move in with relatives to have a roof over their heads or to go back to the old homestead to add to mother's troubles on the farm.

Desperate farmers in the winter of 1932, faced with the loss of their homes, held meetings in country school houses at which old phrases were spoken again, phrases that recalled 1776. "Human rights above contract rights" . . . "Life is more sacred than law." Auctioneers and sheriffs co-operated voluntarily or otherwise at foreclosure sales attended by grim, silent farmers who saw to it that bids were made by the proper persons and by them only. The nation looked on fearfully, unwilling to say that justice did not lie with the embattled farmers.

The story of 1932 is familiar, but the moral may be re-emphasized. The decline in farmers' gross income from 12 billion dollars in 1929 to 5 billion in 1932 was accompanied by a decline in factory payrolls from 11 billion to 5 billion dollars. The shock to the nation's welfare which had been postponed by the artificial device of loans to Europe—the shock which might have been lessened by adjustment of our internal affairs—came with piled up violence when it did come.

And in 1932, there were no cushions to take up the shock. There was no open frontier to take care of surplus labor or bankrupt farmers, no large ready markets abroad to absorb surplus products. The nation's economic processes had become tightly interwoven, from the smallest farm to the largest corporation, from the richest banker to the most penniless unemployed day laborer. What happened at one point was quickly communicated to every other point, and all within a fixed and limited boundary. The nation's problems and mistakes, which it had been able to ignore when it was youthful and expanding, had at last come home. Group problems had become national problems, and could be solved only nationally.

Yet, through 1932, no mechanism had been developed to treat national problems in a national way. 1932 found us back home from our flyer in foreign investments, without either our funds or our markets, with millions in surpluses of goods and labor, with idle factories and breadlines, choked granaries and empty cupboards, stewing in our own juices, suffocated in the midst of plenty.

Now the spirit of the preamble to the Constitution, with its faith in united effort directed toward justice and the common welfare, was needed as badly as it had ever been needed in 1787 or 1858. Moving in this spirit, the people of the United States might meet their common problems by common action. Otherwise they would be defeated by warring pressure groups and narrow legalisms.

Chapter VI

1936, SHAKE HANDS WITH 1787!

ONE hundred and forty-nine years is a short time in the life of a nation. Thanks however to great natural resources and to the industrial revolution, the United States was able to pack the work of perhaps a thousand years of any previous era into the century and a half following 1787. Its occupied land area increased at least twenty times, its population thirty times, and its productivity a hundred-fold.

In 1936 the people of San Francisco are closer to the people of Boston than were the people of Philadelphia in 1787. In some ways, they are closer together than were the people of Lexington and Boston a century and a half ago. A modern Paul Revere with important news to spread would leap to a microphone instead of a horse, and in a few seconds Denver and Los Angeles, as well as Concord and Middlesex, would hear his warning.

The first legislators of the United States figured that a period of about five months was needed between a national election and the convening of the new government, if Congress was to have ample time to get ready and make the journey from its home States to the Capitol. After nearly 150 years, during which time the Senator from Oregon had moved closer to Washington than the Senator from Connecticut had been in 1790, George Norris finally convinced the nation that two months would do instead of five.

In 1936 the people of Chicago eat the same brand of bacon, drive the same automobile and wear the same hats as the people of New York and Seattle. National advertising and chain stores promote a more or less thrilling interest among the people of San Diego and the people of Buffalo in the identical toothpaste and canned soup. The radio and the great press services within a few hours give them domestic and world news from more or less the same angle of interpretation.

The farmers of the great corn, wheat, cotton, tobacco, dairy, fruit and vegetable areas of the United States have come quite generally to realize that their work on the farm is tied in with a great commercial system that includes railroads, commodity exchanges, packing plants, textile mills, wholesale and retail houses, and the pocketbooks of housewives from coast to coast. They have come to know that their welfare is linked up as well with tariffs, international trade balances, and the weather in Argentina and the valley of the Danube.

Workers in automobile, farm-machinery, and textile factories, in steel mills and mines, find their pay envelopes and their jobs affected by a hundred interrelated factors that include the buying power of farmers, the optimism or pessimism of the stock exchange, the ability of young married people to buy new homes, the inventions of new types of machinery, and the decisions of boards of directors of corporations on questions of expansion or contraction of production and the use of surplus funds.

In 1936, only the small farms tucked away in the hollows of the Appalachians and the Ozarks are producing chiefly for home use. The men living on these small farms would understand the way most farmers in 1787 were living, just as they would understand better than any one else the accent and the meaning of words spoken by men in 1787. Strange islands in the commercial seas of 1936, these places where our contemporary great-great-great-grandfathers live! Only in these islands does 1936 shake hands with 1787 on the basis of a common mode of life. I suspect that the people in these isolated spots might agree quite readily, so far as they are concerned, with six members of the Supreme Court who say that agriculture is a local matter.

In 1787, 19 persons on farms were needed to produce enough surplus food to support one person in towns and cities. The farmers of 1787 would be astonished to find 19 persons on farms in 1936 furnishing the necessary food and fiber for 56 persons in cities and 10 people abroad! The farmers of 1787 looked with suspicion on the first iron plows, believing that they would poison the soil. They would gape with astonishment at the binder, the corn husker, the combine and the tractor of a modern farm. Farmers in 1787 thought 30 or 40 miles a rather long distance to send meat from slaughtered animals to market. They would be astonished beyond all measure to discover pork and beef traveling a thousand or more miles to market in 1936.

The artisans of 1787 would be equally astonished by the automatic machinery of a modern factory and by corporations hiring thousands of workers and controlling business in many States.

The statesmen of 1787 were faced with tremendous handicaps in putting across the idea of Federal responsibility under the conditions of the times. Not only was trade and commerce largely local, not only were the people of the several States separated by bad roads, slow communication, unbridged rivers and other physical barriers, but the people were also separated spiritually by their traditions of loyalty to different State sovereignties. Few people in 1787 thought of themselves as "Americans"; they thought of themselves as Virginians, New Yorkers, Pennsylvanians.

Yet the framers of the Constitution were succesful in writing into the enduring law of the land "We the people of the United States," conceiving the nation as a union of people instead of States, and establishing the Federal Government as the instrument of the general welfare.

At no time since the Civil War did Federal responsibility for union in the interest of the general welfare stand out so clearly as in the years of the present depression. Never before had the general welfare been so affected by great, nation-wide economic forces; never before were individuals so helpless to deal with these forces. Even so, the action which the people of the United States needed to take in the face of confusion in 1932 was hardly as drastic as the action the people had taken to meet confusion in 1787, or again in 1861. It was necessary neither to establish a new form of government nor to take up arms against disunion. But it was necessary to recapture the spirit of the statesmen who had founded the Union and the spirit of the nation's greatest leaders in other times of crisis.

President Hoover in 1932 recognized Federal responsibility for many of the problems which had arisen out of the nation's policies during and after the World War. But it was not until 1933 that the Government was able to take really energetic action. In that year the nation sought to meet nationally its national responsibilities. It is not my purpose here to defend in detail the actions taken or draw lessons from mistakes made. What stands out clearly, however, is that world affairs since the war, and especially since 1930, have been such that the United States, like every other nation, has found it absolutely necessary to shoulder a vast amount of national responsibility.

Great concentration of economic power in the hands of a relatively few corporations, brilliant success in the mass production of goods of all kinds coupled with a rather dismal failure in distributing those goods continuously on a wide scale, technological unemployment, exploitation of the country's resources to the point where the problem of conservation is serious, complex international relations: these are the problems we have to meet today just as in 1787 the nation had to meet the problems of separate State sovereignties, confusion in money and tariff matters, and general chaos resulting from a weak national government under the Articles of Confederation.

The statesmen of 1787 were amazingly resourceful and daring in establishing a national mechanism with which to deal with their national problems. They frankly disregarded the letter of previous law, and created an entirely new instrument to take the place of the Articles of Confederation. I am inclined to think—though speculation of this sort is quite fruitless—that Madison, Franklin and the others, faced with our complicated problems today, would consider our efforts toward solution decidedly timid and lacking in sweep.

They would certainly recognize one very familiar issue that faces us today as it faced them in 1787. This is the question as to which problems are local in nature and which are federal in nature. As the statesmen of 1787 assumed that many of the problems of their day were federal in nature, so the administration under Franklin Roosevelt assumed that many of the problems of 1933 were federal in nature. Effective action of any sort required this primary assumption. The action taken in 1933, while much less drastic than the action taken in 1787, was dramatic and swift, and resulted in improved conditions.

Later, however, it was found that not all the groups and makers of opinion in the country were in agreement with the administration on this question of local and federal powers. The same thing had been true in 1787. Many historians, in fact, believe that a purely popular vote in 1787 would have rejected the principle of federalism as incorporated in the Constitution. Only after a good deal of high-pressure salesmanship was the Constitution accepted.

In 1933, the situation seems rather more favorable to Federalism than it was in 1787. According to a vote taken by the Institute of Public Opinion, 56 percent of the people agree that the Federal Government should have right of way over State governments. Only the large corporations, the Republican Party, New England, the Liberty League, and most of the newspapers of the country are apparently for States' rights today at any cost.

To these sections, interests and groups, however, must be added one other body, at least part of the time. The Supreme Court has disagreed in a number of instances with the position taken by the administration on the matter of federal powers. In the case of the NRA it held that the commerce clause of the

Constitution did not give the Federal Government
the powers it had assumed to set up rules for business. In the case of the AAA, it held that agriculture
was a local matter, and that its regulation, whether or
not in the interests of the general welfare, is a power
not granted to the Federal Government but reserved
to the States under the tenth amendment.*

There may have been much in these acts and in
their administration which was unwise. But the
grounds taken by the Supreme Court in invalidating
them raise a most fundamental question as to the
ability of our form of government at crucial times to
meet nationally the problems that have become
national in scope.

To interpret the Constitution in the light of the
spirit of its framers is one thing. To interpret it in
the light of economic conditions as they were in
1787 when the Constitution was drawn up is another.
I do not doubt that through the multiplicity of legal
precedents available to the Supreme Court it is
possible to take a narrow view of the Constitution
which virtually limits the scope of granted federal
powers to those which would have seemed useful
under the conditions of 1787. Other legal precedents,
I believe, permit a broader view. The Supreme Court
in the AAA decision, it seems to me, chose to interpret the Constitution in the light of a handicraft

---

* Since this was written, the Guffey Act designed to stabilize conditions in the bituminous coal industry, has also been declared unconstitutional on similar grounds.

age when it took 19 farmers to produce enough surplus food for only one city person, rather than in the
light of modern machinery which enables 19 people
on farms to produce for 56 city people and 10 living
abroad—and, when foreign markets disappear, to
pile up tremendous surpluses besides. In this decision I do not believe that the Supreme Court interpreted the Constitution in the spirit of the founding
fathers who were concerned for unity and the general
welfare under an effective Federal Government.

Were agriculture truly a local matter in 1936, as
the Supreme Court says it is, half of the people of
the United States would quickly starve. Were
commerce actually limited to what takes place
within State borders, three-fourths of business and
industry would be dead or crippled, and our great
corporations would be bankrupt.

The doctrine of States' rights, now invoked by the
Supreme Court, was a barrier to progress even in
1787, and was the cause of terrible conflict in 1861.
Today, the States mark no economic boundaries that
make sense, and they provide only limited instruments for action to meet modern problems. Long ago
the great corporations managed to break down
States' rights when they interfered with corporate
expansion. Today it is clear that States' rights are
being invoked not for the rights which they defend,
but for privileges they protect. They are being invoked by groups which have already obtained
centralizing powers under government, but which

by this means seek to prevent extension of centralizing power to other groups, such as farmers and
labor.

Except for a small number of farm families living
in isolated mountain valleys, we in 1936 cannot shake
hands with 1787 on the basis of the way we live and
produce and exchange goods. The 6 million farm
families who sell 85 percent of their produce to
people living in cities and towns, the 25 million city
families who must obtain this produce if they are to
survive away from the land, the 90 percent of the
wage earners who work for corporations, and all of
us who as consumers depend every day on goods and
services which derive from all parts of the continent
and from foreign nations, have little in common
economically with the self-sufficing farmers, artisans,
small merchants and land-owning professional people
of 1787.

We can, however, shake hands with 1787 on the
basis of common spiritual aims. The men of 1787
provide us with a high goal to strive for in the
courage and imagination with which they faced the
problem of the general welfare. Literal application
of the details of the Constitution which they bequeathed to us, if interpreted without recognition of
the profound changes one hundred and forty-nine
years have brought about, may result in the most
terrible disaster. But interpretation of the Constitution in the light of the purposes of its framers, as
revealed in the preamble, will make it a living

instrument of progress. Our task is to work with our present materials and under present conditions so as to build in our day the more perfect union which the men of 1787 conceived, and through a more perfect union to establish justice and promote the general welfare. Thus and only thus may 1936 shake hands in true good faith with 1787.

Part Two

THE GENERAL WELFARE TODAY

Chapter VII

"THE BLESSINGS OF LIBERTY"

LIBERTY has always been a ringing word to the people of the United States. In the Declaration of Independence liberty rang out at a high and clarion pitch, and twelve years later, in the preamble to the Constitution, it was necessary for the statesmen of the new nation to mingle the notes of unity and inter-dependence with the note of liberty in order that a more harmonious chord might be struck to guide the destiny of the country.

Nevertheless, the Blessings of Liberty were dear and real to the hearts of our ancestors, so that they were written deep not only in the preamble to the Constitution, but in the whole structure of the new instrument of government, and then further and specifically enumerated in the articles of the Bill of Rights. Liberty to the early patriots meant personal and civil rights. It meant liberty of conscience and speech; it meant the divorce of the State from other institutions which should belong to the people—church and press and educational practices. It meant the right to assemble freely and speak freely and be safe from arbitrary action by the State as had been common under more autocratic forms of government.

The men who wrote the Constitution did not think

of liberty as applying particularly to property and property rights. They were sufficiently concerned about property rights; many of them were anxious that the new government under the Constitution would make good the depreciated currency and securities that they held and protect their interests in real property by firm laws of contract. But when they asked for validation of debts, securities and paper money, they asked for Justice rather than Liberty, and they took care to insure that justice to property and finance would be done through the various contract clauses of the Constitution and the prohibition against State issuance of money. Property was mostly real property at the time, held by individuals. Corporate property was almost unknown. Capital had not accumulated in very large masses either in the hands of individuals or in the hands of commercial companies.

During the latter half of the nineteenth century, when the great expansion of industry and finance took place, industrialists and financiers began to talk less about justice for property and more about liberty for property, and by property they meant large capital enterprises. The Blessings of Liberty, in their minds, became interfused with the philosophy of laissez-faire capitalism which was being popularized by the Manchester school of economics, and this concept began to influence even the decisions of justices of the Supreme Court. Many cases in which the rights of capital were involved were won under interpretations which glossed the clauses of the Constitution relating to liberty so that they seemed to mean freedom of capital to pursue profits without regulation by either State or Federal Governments.

The industrialists who were now invoking "liberty" so enthusiastically were not thinking particularly about the rights to free speech, free assembly and free worship, the blessings of which the early patriots were so anxious to insure. In fact, these same capitalists often used strong-arm methods and obtained injunctions from the courts to prevent workers or other opposing groups from exercising their civil rights.

The gradual changing of the meaning of Blessings of Liberty in the minds of wealthy Americans from personal and civil rights to sanctification of the methods of big business is something that would have astonished the framers of the Constitution. Yet by 1934, this new meaning of liberty had become so fixed in the minds of some people that a group of large capitalists and corporation lawyers, representing in the aggregate some billions of dollars of private and corporate wealth, could form a quasi-political association under the name "The Liberty League" in the assumption that such a title properly described the interests they wished to defend.

Every one sincerely interested in the welfare of the United States at the present time must be concerned more than ever to defend the Blessings of

Liberty in the sense of the civil rights which the framers of the Constitution wanted to insure. When the nation is faced with deep-lying economic problems which call for courageous thinking and action it is more than ever important that people be free to reason realistically about these problems and give expression to every shade of thought and opinion. When distress is still widespread, it is important more than ever that there be no curtailment of the civil rights of any group, for there is no greater threat to orderly government and orderly change than the driving underground of forces of discontent and disaffection.

Though local instances of civil injustice unfortunately occur in America, I believe no nation on the whole believes more strongly in civil freedom today than the United States. Many nations have rejected civil freedom almost entirely. There are forces in the United States, too, which seek to restrict civil freedom, often in the name of a jingo "Americanism." I believe the common sense of the people of the United States is quite capable of discounting and defeating these forces, whether in their threat to academic freedom, to the rights of minority groups, or to other democratic rights and processes.

The greatest threat to liberty in the United States lies in the very excess of that kind of liberty which puts great economic power in a few private hands. Economic liberty is never won and fixed forever; its benefits continually tend to gravitate toward the stronger or shrewder elements of society, leaving other elements with little or no liberty. Society must ever be alert to renew economic liberty on a broader pattern, for if left too long uncontrolled, economic liberty becomes economic autocracy, and almost always results at last in some kind of political despotism. A situation in which the 36 thousand families at the top of the economic pyramid get as much income as the 12 million families at the bottom is a dangerous situation so far as maintaining true liberty is concerned.

Liberty, now as in 1787, must be harmonized with justice and the general welfare, if it is to promote a healthy condition in society for its own preservation. Otherwise it is only a false front for privilege, and courts its own destruction.

"Liberty of opportunity" is a brave American slogan which brought millions of people from the Old World to seek their fortune in the New. When there was plenty of elbow room in America, when opportunities of all sorts were open to every one in a rapidly expanding country, this slogan rang out clearly and meant something. Now, however, when it is fondly repeated by our more fortunate people, it has a hollow sound to the millions of American people whose opportunity for jobs and livelihood is practically non-existent. "Liberty of opportunity" is not automatic in a country whose frontiers are closed and in which 90 percent of jobs in industry are controlled by corporations.

The United States still has greater resources in relation to its population than perhaps any other country on earth. "Liberty of opportunity" should and can be still a reality. But the relationship between freedom and economic opportunity has undergone great changes with changing economic conditions here and abroad, and no one has a right to talk about "liberty of opportunity" in America today unless he has some program for meeting these changes and making this liberty real.

Freedom for the machine and for the corporate form of organization, whatever benefits they have brought, has resulted under the present rules of the game in great limitations upon the freedom and opportunity of many groups of people. Freedom to produce unlimited quantities of foodstuffs does not spell economic opportunity to farmers whose foreign markets have disappeared through changed international conditions and whose income from domestic sales depends on activity and wages in industry. Complete freedom of initiative, too, when given modern machinery and operating under intensive competition, has fallen with great force on our physical resources of minerals and soil, and threatens to limit very much the freedom and economic opportunity of future generations who will inherit these abused resources.

Our problem today is to make the adjustments necessary in our social mechanisms so that we will have social controls where they are needed to enlarge the field of economic opportunity for people as a whole. Only thus may "liberty of opportunity" once more become a reality instead of a hollow precept or the luxury of privileged groups. The purpose of the next few chapters is to examine some of the changes that have taken place in economic conditions and in our relations with the rest of the world which must be taken into account if we are to provide a broader economic basis for our cherished Blessings of Liberty.

Chapter VIII

SOIL AND THE GENERAL WELFARE

OF ALL the circumstances which have combined to make this nation different from the nations of the Old World, rich soil and plenty of it, free or nearly so to all comers, stands first. Freeholders in a wide land of fabulous fertility, guarded by great oceans from foreign invasion, could erect separate strongholds of individual enterprise, free speech and free conscience. In no spread-eagle sense, but in plain truth, liberty and equality have been a natural outgrowth of our great gift of soil.

But the dynamic quality which characterizes civilized man does not leave such a gift unmodified. If nature was prodigal with us, we have been ten times more prodigal with her. During the past 150 years, we white men have destroyed more soil, timber and wild-life than the Indians, left to themselves, would have destroyed in many thousands of years.

If we allow the original rich gift of soil which has been the foundation of so much of our liberties and privileges to keep washing and wearing thinner, what of the ultimate crop? Can we greatly diminish the basis of our life in the soil, and still save our liberties? If we, as a people, through enlightened and

SOIL AND THE GENERAL WELFARE   107

voluntary measures do not co-operate to protect our heritage of soil, may we not be said in part to have willfully undermined our own foundations?

It is easy to excuse the farmers of one hundred years ago for the way in which they mismanaged their farms. In the first place most of them didn't know there was such a thing as soil erosion. There was available very little scientific knowledge about methods of soil building or of avoiding soil depletion. In the second place, in a land so vast with population so thin, the easiest course oftentimes was to wear out a farm and then move on west. No one worries about conserving the air. Why should any one give a thought to saving the land when there is plenty of it?

On the basis of their record it would be easy to indict the people of the United States as killers, looters and exploiters. Several species of wild life have completely disappeared, others have been greatly reduced, and fish cannot live in many of our streams because of pollution. We have wastefully slashed down our forests and have exploited our oil and mineral resources. Pastures and hillsides have been plowed. But in all of this I am convinced that the American people were thoughtless rather than willfully destructive. They were victims of the customs of the immediate past, when the important thing was to fill up a continent with people as rapidly as possible, even though the result might be exploitation rather than conservation.

Today we have come to a time when the continuation of the exploitive frame of mind can easily be disastrous. Already we have allowed erosion by water to destroy more than 50 million acres, representing an area equal to all of the arable land in New York and Pennsylvania. Another 50 million acres have been damaged almost to the point of ruination for productive use, and an additional 100 million acres have been seriously impoverished. The process of erosion is rapidly gaining headway on still another 100 million acres, some of it the most valuable farm land remaining in the United States. Wind erosion has nearly ruined four million acres and is active on about 60 million acres, largely in the High Plains regions. People who have not studied the results of investigations made at soil erosion experiment stations in central and western United States cannot appreciate how terribly real is soil erosion. At these stations arrangements are made for carefully weighing the soil which is removed from the land by the rain under different systems of cropping. On many slopes, one exceedingly hard rain will remove as much as an inch of soil from land in corn or in cotton.

Western Europeans accustomed to rains which are much gentler in nature and with a much smaller percentage of their land in clean tilled crops cannot understand the extreme seriousness of the erosion problem of the United States. Hundreds of thousands of our farmers were either born in western Europe themselves or come from parents or grandparents born in western Europe. They have not, therefore, been trained in traditions which would take into account the soil erosion factor. Nearly half of our land is farmed by tenants who stay on the average only two or three years on the same farm and whose chief concern is getting together enough money to pay the rent this particular year. The landlords, on the other hand, are driven by the necessity of getting enough money out of the land to pay the taxes and interest on the mortgage and they oftentimes have only slightly more interest in the land than the tenants. In other words it would seem that on at least a million farms the landlords and tenants are forced by their economic situation to enter into a conspiracy which in effect promotes erosion rather than prevents it.

People in cities may forget the soil for as long as a hundred years, but mother nature's memory is long and she will not let them forget indefinitely. The soil is the mother of man and if we forget her, life eventually weakens. George Washington and Thomas Jefferson sensed this at a time when land was superabundant and the pioneers were still prodigal in their wasting. Jefferson, on his first farm about five miles from Charlottesville in central Virginia, tried to stop the soil washing off his sloping fields by plowing around the hills instead of up and down. He is said to have been the first man in the United States to promote this type of plowing. Doubtless the system helps some, but today we have come to under-

stand that no single measure of land treatment used
alone is adequate to combat erosion. The first farm
of Jefferson's is today a ruined monument to the destructive powers of erosion.

Both Washington and Jefferson were strong believers in rotation as a method of preserving soil fertility and Washington when he was away from home
sent a number of letters to his farm manager advocating certain rotation plans. In his last message to
Congress, Washington stated that "with reference
either to individual or national welfare, agriculture
is of primary importance," and he urged the establishment of a Federal bureau to advance agriculture.
Both Washington and Jefferson were far in advance
of the people of their time.

When the cotton gin came into extensive use there
began in the South an expansion of the cotton crop
which resulted in the destruction of millions of
acres of plow land in southeastern United States.
When machinery was invented for the more rapid
plowing, disking and cultivating of corn land, the
farmers in parts of the Middle West entered upon a
period of promoting soil erosion which put the farmers of the Southeast to shame as mere beginners in
the art of soil exploitation. At the time of the World
War tractors and combines came into the picture.
Millions of acres of pasture were plowed. In the hu-
mid parts of the grain belt the sloping fields became
greatly subject to erosion, and in the drier parts
wind erosion became a serious problem, especially

during March and April of the drier years. Drainage
became an obsession, at the same time that the grass
was plowed. Rivers were straightened, and the spring
and summer rains were sent to the sea with the greatest possible speed. Lake levels and water tables
dropped. Underground water reserves declined to a
point which made it almost impossible to obtain well
water in many farm areas when the dry seasons came
along.

If the climate shifts to the dry side, dust storms,
failing wells and lack of subsoil moisture will become
an exceedingly serious problem in many areas. If the
climate shifts to the wet side, the excess of drainage
will not prove at all embarrassing but the planting
of too much land in crops will result in sending the
surface soil either to silt up the streams or to move on
to the ocean.

Yes, the white man is learning that in a land with
a continental climate of high winds and sudden dash-
ing rains and rather violent extremes of weather from
one year to the next, it is the part of wisdom to
leave a higher percentage of the land in grass and
trees than has been the custom in the United States
so far.

As this book was being written, there occurred in
the eastern part of the United States possibly the
worst and most widespread floods in its history—
those of the spring of 1936. These floods were of
course the result of an unusually severe winter, during which heavy snows piled up in the watersheds and

the ground was so deeply frozen in many areas that it could not absorb the water when the snows melted in the spring. While the actions of man were not chiefly responsible for these floods, undoubtedly they contributed to the excessive degree of damage done. I happened to visit an experiment station on one of the headwaters of the Susquehanna shortly after the period of the floods, at which time ground conditions were much the same as during the floods. There I learned that, during a week when 5 inches of rain fell, a plot of cleared or plowed ground lost 50 percent of the rainfall in the form of run-off, while on a plot covered with trees and the usual amount of forest litter, there was no loss by run-off. The explanation of the greater power of the forest land to hold back the rainfall seemed to be that the forest litter served not only as an absorbent in itself, but also protected the ground from freezing, and thus made it capable of holding the water, while the cleared land, without such protection, was frozen to the point where it shed most of the water. Undoubtedly the destruction of forests and the excessive clearing and plowing of hillside and mountain lands hastened the rush of waters into the rivers and contributed to the severity of the floods.

The floods of March, 1936, made millions of city people conscious of the need for better management of the headwaters of our great rivers. Part of the problem is the erection of dams, reservoirs and levees; part of it is reforestation; and another important part is the holding of the soil in place on individual farms. In fact, engineering structures without simultaneous corrective action taken by the owners of land in the watershed may be made useless in a relatively short time because of the filling up of reservoirs through deposit of silt.

The life of a flourishing civilization demands recognition by landowners and the National Government of the necessity of co-operating in behalf of the general welfare to prevent soil erosion and floods. This problem runs across State lines.

We may well take a lesson from northwestern China and Asia Minor. It took several hundred years for the people of these lands to reduce them to deserts. We in the United States are moving faster because we have the advantage of machinery. Thus far the damage has not been completely ruinous, but in another thirty or forty years we may do irreparable harm.

Probably the most damaging indictment that can be made of the capitalistic system is the way in which its emphasis on unfettered individualism results in exploitation of natural resources in a manner to destroy the physical foundations of national longevity. Is there no way for the capitalistic system to develop a mechanism for taking thought and planning action in terms of the general welfare for the long run as represented by the conservation of soil and other natural resources which are being competitively exploited?

The experience of Sweden would seem to suggest that excessive exploitation can be avoided, if the competitive spirit is restrained by reasonable regulatory laws and if the nation does a certain amount of national planning for the general welfare. Sweden has long led the world in the care and maintenance of its forest resources, and more recently has pursued an enlightened policy with respect to other natural resources, such as mines and water-power. As long ago as 1600 it passed its first national forest law and in 1752 it surveyed its land resources and reserved large forest areas for national conservation and development. Now its forest laws require that all industries and persons engaged in timber cutting must replace the timber removed within a reasonable length of time and that no forest lands be left bare or unplanted with good new stock. In the case of mining industries, Sweden requires that private companies look to the long-time welfare of the people dependent on these industries by establishing welfare funds which can take care of workers and their families after the mines have been exhausted in any given locality. Sweden's efforts prove that a nation's natural resources may be used with regard to the long-time general welfare, rather than exploited merely for temporary profits. The United States is many years behind Sweden in this respect and might well profit from its example.

So far as soil resources are concerned, however, the problem is related to the business cycle and to unem-

ployment in the cities as well as to practices of farming in themselves. For example, between 1930 and
1934 about two million young people were raised on
the farm who normally would have gone to the cities
but who stayed at home to go into the farming business. Largely as a result of these two million young
people backed up on the farm, five hundred thousand
new farms came into existence between 1930 and
1935. Many of these new farms are on hilly land and
poor soil. The young people are certain to eke out a
miserable existence on this poor land and the land is
certain to be harmed.

Thus the soil problem is urban as well as rural. If
city industry were to proceed at its normal rate of
activity, it could absorb the excess young people
from the farms and put them to work doing things
much more profitable for the general welfare of the
United States than the cultivation of land which
ought to be in grass and trees. Nevertheless, I am convinced it is better for the young people of the farms
to eke out a miserable existence on poor soil than to
come to the cities to burden the relief rolls or sit
around in idleness.

But it is not only the desperate farming of poverty-
stricken individuals, burdened by the necessity of
selling crops at low prices to pay rents, taxes or mort-
gages, that destroys the land. Large scale lumber-
men, cattle-men and grain farmers are almost equally
responsible. Big men as well as little men are soil
destroyers. Sometimes the local or State taxation

policy forces exploitation, especially in timber. Yes, we are all of us guilty in one way or another of neglecting the soil or fostering its exploitation in a manner which may prove to be exceedingly embarrassing for our children and grandchildren. Should regulatory methods be adopted? In some cases, yes, but in other cases it may be necessary to offer financial incentive to induce individuals to act in the public interest.

Under the Agricultural Adjustment Administration there were financial incentives for shifting millions of acres of farm land producing crops no longer needed (crops which were hard on the soil) into soil-enriching legumes and soil-binding grasses. The new Conservation and Allotment Act, we believe, will promote such shifts on an even broader and more permanent basis. Under the Soil Conservation Service needed experiments are being carried out and technical aid and services given to help farmers in 41 States to prevent erosion and remedy soil wastage on 141 damaged watershed areas. The Resettlement Administration is making readjustments of the use of land too poor for farming and helping families to find better land or occupation. The Tennessee Valley Authority is trying to control erosion and bad land practices in the entire watershed of the Tennessee River which embraces parts of seven States. These various programs are steps in the direction of wiser use and protection of our resources. But all of these

efforts will be inadequate until we solve the problem
of farm tenancy and the problem of unemployment,
the twin problems of human erosion which strike so
deeply into the heart of our national life. It is no
mere figure of speech to say that we will not get rid
of soil erosion until we also get rid of human erosion.

From the scientific point of view we have perhaps
thirty years in which to make the key decision which
will determine whether or not we shall be able to
maintain our soil on a fertile, self-renewing basis.
But from the standpoint of human psychology, the
key decision may be made within the next five or
ten years or perhaps within the next two or three.
Much depends, in fact, on the way in which farmers
are able to co-operate with one another and with the
State experiment stations and the Federal Department of Agriculture in making the new Soil Conservation program work during 1936, 1937 and 1938.
Much also depends on the way in which those in the
cities develop a feeling of responsibility for the soil
as the foundation of their existence as well as the
existence of farmers. The cities have become increasingly aware of the soil problem because of such striking catastrophes as dust storms and floods, but so
far this interest has been rather superficial. It is
difficult for city people to visualize the slow processes
of erosion that are going on every day, which are not
as spectacular, but actually more damaging, than
sudden dust storms or floods. It is also difficult for

them to understand the problem of slow depletion of soil fertility through continuous removal of crops without replenishment of the soil by proper rotation.

There is a practical long-time solution to the problem of maintaining soil resources with which the scientists are becoming increasingly familiar. Will the newspapers, the radio and the schools do their part in carrying that scientific knowledge to farmers and city people alike? If this task is well done, even the most thoughtless individuals will not object to the continuing use of governmental power to regulate exploitation on the one hand and to furnish scientific assistance and financial incentive on the other to bring about the gradual and permanent shift of our excess plow land to grass and trees. Will the farmers and the cities learn to work together to build a self-renewing soil and a self-renewing civilization?

Chapter IX

POPULATION AND THE GENERAL
WELFARE

THE welfare and longevity of a nation depend on the natural resources available to it, the people that make it up, and the traditions the people live by. Rich natural resources in themselves may prove of little lasting advantage if the population of a nation deteriorates and its traditions decay. The factors that influence population should be the subject of profound research and have the thoughtful attention of men in public affairs and every one concerned with the nation's welfare.

The changing make-up of population in the United States has an importance which perhaps not one person out of a thousand recognizes and appreciates. Extraordinary shifts are taking place in the numerical relationship between young and old people, between farm and city people and between privileged and under-privileged groups. These changes will have a most surprising effect upon the make-up of the nation ten, twenty and a hundred years hence. Many of these effects can be foreseen, and if they are foreseen and taken into account, statesmanlike action can prevent disastrous consequences. If the changes are not recognized and prepared for, but are allowed to steal upon us unaware, permanent harm may be done to our most cherished values and traditions, and politicians may be faced with forces and conditions with which they can no longer deal constructively.

The outstanding fact about population in the United States today is that our birth rate has been going down so rapidly since 1921 that we may anticipate the peak of our population to be reached at around 145 million or less in the year 1950. From then on there is reason to fear that our population may slowly begin to decline. Recognition of this possibility should lead to certain readjustments in our economic and social policies if the nation's welfare is to be promoted.

The levelling off of our population means in the first place that the percentage of younger people in the nation is declining and the percentage of older people increasing. This trend has been strikingly evident through the 1920's, when the number of people over 65 years increased 34 percent for the nation as a whole and 50 percent for the urban population. If this trend continues, as we have reason to believe, twenty-five years from now there will be twice as many old people as there are today.

Thoughtful students of such trends as this in the make-up of our population are able to foresee various situations which should be prepared for, if the nation is not to get into trouble. In the near future, for example, the number of married people in our population will probably increase rather strikingly, so that by 1946, there will be some seven million more married people than there are today. Perhaps two-thirds of these seven million additional married people will need new houses. Undoubtedly this demand will create a building boom some time during the period from 1937 to 1947.

Some years thereafter, however, as a result of the smaller number of children born from 1930 to 1935, there will be a decline in the number of people marrying. Unless at that time there should be a great change in the type of dwelling and an improved standard of living which should enable people to junk old houses and buy new ones, there should be a considerable decline in the demand for new houses. If Dr. O. E. Baker of the Department of Agriculture, from whom most of these figures have been obtained, is correct in his analysis, it is possible that the depression in the building trades which will begin some ten or twenty years from now, may be even more serious than that which extended from 1930 to 1935. Unless we are prepared in advance for such a depression following on the heels of a great boom, we shall run into the same sort of confusion as we did in the early '30s with perhaps even more serious social consequences.

The increase in the percentage of older people and the decline in the percentage of younger people will lead to other situations for which we should be prepared. Colleges training young people for the teaching profession, for example, should be prepared to taper off the number of candidates for high school teaching after the next five years, and the number of candidates for college teaching after the next ten years. As the percentage of older people in our population increases, educational bodies may well consider expanding activities devoted to adult education.

Other groups, too, should be prepared to meet increasingly the needs of older people. The building trades might be able to cushion in some degree the shock of a housing depression ten or twenty years from now by developing apartment houses and smaller dwellings attractive to older people, especially in such regions as California and Florida. Some program for maintaining the buying power of our more elderly people is indicated as a social and economic necessity for the future welfare of the nation.

A fact which has even more bearing on the future welfare of the country than the shift in age groups is the striking difference in birth rates between urban and rural groups. The people in the cities do not have enough children to replace themselves. At the present time ten adults in the cities are having about seven children. When these seven are grown, it is probable they will have about five, and the five in turn will have but three or four children. In other words, were it not for the fact that the population of the cities can be replenished by people from the farms, the city population would fall in a hundred years to one-third of its present level.

Within the cities there is another difference in birth rates. People with higher incomes have fewer children than those with lower incomes. We do not know enough about eugenics to judge whether stocks from different classes or groups are more desirable to society than those from other classes or groups, and if we did know it might be difficult or even unwise to use the knowledge. But we do know enough about the influence of environment and education on human beings to realize that it is of the greatest importance that the breeding grounds of the future population have economic and cultural advantages commensurate with their potential influence on the nation's destiny.

This means that better education and housing and medical care for the people living in crowded sections of cities where the birth rate is high are not simply matters of justice to these people. They are matters of plain common sense for society as a whole. A better distribution of income and of social advantages is insurance not only against crime and disease today but against an unstable and ill-prepared society tomorrow.

Of even greater importance to the nation's future welfare are the conditions of life for the children of farm people. One thousand farm people today will in all probability have about seven times the number of descendants a hundred years from now as a thousand city people will have. Putting it another way probably more than two-thirds of the people living

in the United States in the year 2036 will be de-
scended from those who today are living on farms,
and only one-third from those living in cities. This
is in spite of the fact that the farm population is now
only one-fourth of the city population.

In a literal sense, the land produces the life-stream
of the nation. The cities cannot live unto themselves
even in a purely population sense. Their stock must
be continually replenished by young people bred on
the farms.

This contribution of the farms to the cities has an
economic aspect which very few city people perhaps
appreciate. The country rears and educates young
people about half of whom will later contribute their
energies and talents to the cities. During the 1920's,
some 6 million people from the farms, over two-thirds
of whom were less than 25 years of age, migrated to
the cities. Their up-bringing represented perhaps 14
billion dollars worth of care and education, a sum
equal to the value of all the wheat crops and nearly
half of the cotton crops produced during the decade.
This cost, which had been assumed by farm parents,
was a contribution to the welfare of the cities.

There is no essential conflict of interests here.
Farmers in turn benefit from the activities in the
cities which their own children help to advance.
The concentration of people and wealth in cities
makes possible certain social and cultural as well as
economic activities—music, drama, the spread of
ideas—which cannot be facilitated as readily in the

country, but from which people in the country benefit. Concentration of people and wealth in the cities
sometimes goes too far, so that a counter-movement
of decentralization, "back to the land," is needed.
It is not necessary to debate the ultimate or exclu-
sive benefits of one or the other way of life. Both
are needed in a well-balanced society. But city
people may well ponder on the fact that their own
welfare is affected in a direct and literal sense by
the welfare of people in the country. Impoverish-
ment of farm life means a lesser or poorer contribution of farm life to city life. Only if people on the
farms have the income and advantages necessary to
rear capable and well-trained children is the welfare
of the nation as a whole assured.

The United States in earlier years, when immigration brought hundreds of thousands of young people
into the country every year and when opportunities
of all sorts were open in the newer parts of the country, did not have to plan consciously with regard to
its problems of population. Now, however, with
frontiers closed, immigration virtually ended and
the population levelling off, it is of great importance
that the problems of population be anticipated and
dealt with. As the percentage of older people increases, there is grave danger of a spirit of fatalism
and defeatism overtaking the country such as exists
in some older countries. This is especially likely to
occur if our society does not offer training and opportunities to young people which will stimulate their

ambitions and nourish their hopes, and if it does not
offer security for older people which will give them an
adequate economic stake in society.

Undoubtedly the solution of the problems raised
by a changing make-up of population will mean more
conscious planning along certain lines. Adjustments
as between certain occupations and in the settlement of certain groups of people will become more
necessary, and such adjustments will not be automatic, but must be planned and facilitated by society itself. In some degree it may be desirable to
promote decentralization of industries from the large
cities, so that more workers have access to the open
country—a trend upon which many industrialists
look with favor. Opportunities for greater use of our
resources and for an increase in many services needed
by society are not limited either by our resources or
by our needs. They are limited by our unwillingness
to deal socially with social problems. Above all, the
nation must be concerned that its breeding stock is
taken care of, that the nation does not deteriorate
at the source of its life-blood, which is in the land.

Chapter X

FOREIGN TRADE AND THE GENERAL
WELFARE

SINCE the World War the general welfare of the United States has been affected by world conditions to a greater degree than at any other time in our history. The World War brought about a revolution in our relations with foreign nations. It found us owing them some 3 billion dollars; it left us with a net credit of some 15 billion dollars. No study of our domestic welfare since the war can ignore the problems growing out of this changed relationship.

The nineteenth century and early part of the twentieth was a golden age for world trade. An unusually favorable relationship existed between developed and undeveloped nations, between nations with finished products to sell and nations with raw materials to sell. Exchange of goods between nations in this situation was easy to finance and mutually profitable to promote.

Undeveloped nations, however, do not remain undeveloped forever. They bring in machinery and learn to produce many things which they previously imported. The spread of machinery and power tends to equalize the differences between nations and tends to decrease the range of dissimilar products which it is profitable to exchange.

This process was hastened by the World War, when nations outside Europe speeded up industrial activities of all sorts. Since the war, there has been an almost psychopathic desire on the part of many nations to become as self-sufficient as possible. Subsidies for domestic producers have been common, and restraints upon imports have been imposed. Nations are glad to sell abroad, but they don't want to buy. This means that both buying and selling between nations diminish, for over a period of time no nation can sell without buying. Nations all over the world have caught the disease of nationalism.

The disease is contagious. How far it has spread can be seen by examining what the nations of the world have been doing with respect to production, marketing and foreign trade in agricultural products.

Great Britain finds it a good policy to strengthen trade between herself and her empire countries. She turns to these countries for wheat, meat, dairy products, cotton and fruits, and asks these countries to take their pay in British manufactured goods. Also, the British Government pays subsidies to British farmers and sets up import quotas on food from the rest of the world. Germany has a widespread farm control system which regulates both production and marketing, and forces processors and handlers into compulsory unions. France pays a bonus to persons who produce wheat and limits imports by quotas.

Italy pays subsidies on silk and rice, stimulates her wheat production enormously, and requires farmers to use their land efficiently or be dispossessed. Holland substitutes wheat for forage crops and does away with surplus dairy cows. Denmark adjusts the bacon supply. Argentina uses exchange controls to market her surplus wheat at a satisfactory price. Brazil has a coffee valorization plan, which since 1930 has required the destruction of coffee surpluses equivalent to the world's consumption for one and a half years.

What is the net effect of all these artificial devices? It might seem, on first glance, that it is a good thing for every nation to stimulate its own production and cut down imports from other countries. If more countries grew their own wheat and meats, it would seem, there would be more food to share. Actually, however, it works the other way. A nation which forces production of things it is not fitted to produce must drop production of things it is fitted to produce. Germany, for example, forces her production of foodstuffs; but because she imports less food she exports less of other things. The resulting paralysis of industry destroys the domestic market for foodstuffs. After having produced foods at high prices, the grower must sell them at low prices, or have the Government pay the difference out of the pockets of consumers.

As one nation adopts this policy, other nations are forced to adopt similar policies. When their export of things they are fitted to produce is cut off they, too, must take to producing other things which they are less fitted to produce. The result is that many nations shift from producing efficiently to producing inefficiently, and this means a loss in total production and a decrease in the total wealth to be shared.

The United States, if necessary, could play the nationalistic game as well or better than any other nation. We could very nearly get along without imports if we had to. We now need to bring in rubber, certain rare metals and tropical products, but in a pinch we could learn to produce our own rubber, could do without tropical products, and our chief absolute necessity to be imported would be a rather small quantity of rare metals.

But the United States, like every other nation, would have to make drastic internal readjustments in order to get on a strict nationalistic basis. One-tenth of all we produce we normally sell abroad. Among certain groups and in certain sections the percentage of our people dependent on international trade is very high. Normally over half of our cotton and 40 percent of our tobacco are sold abroad. The cotton belt, especially the western half, would feel acutely the removal of its export trade. Going nationalistic would mean training a good many people who now produce cotton, tobacco, wheat, hogs and automobiles to produce sugar cane in Louisiana, beet sugar in the Far West and guayule for rubber in the Southwest.

Would we be better off if we re-educated the 10 percent or so of our people who produce and handle our exports to produce and handle a variety of new products as substitutes for our imports? It might take a good many years of shortage and hardship before we could get the new industries going well. And even then we couldn't produce sugar as cheaply as farmers in Cuba and the Philippines produce it, and rubber produced in the United States would probably cost three or four times as much as rubber produced in the East Indies or South America. Besides, our people would have to be deprived entirely of such tropical products as coffee and cocoa if we were to become purely self-sufficient.

Furthermore, great hardship and social unrest would result in Cuba, the Philippines and other countries dependent on the United States for their trade, if we cut off imports from them. We would be held responsible for this situation before the bar of world public opinion.

Foreign trade, however, has long been conducted by all countries in a rather ruthless and immoral fashion. It has been considered good practice by companies which have a large domestic business to handle their export surpluses in such a way as to maintain domestic prices, but without any regard for the effect of their export sales on the world price situation. In some countries, export products are sweated out of labor getting five cents an hour or less in order that the products can be put on the world market at cut-rate prices. From the standpoint of long-time world trade health it seems obvious that everything should be done to discourage the world movement of goods when it means cut-throat competition and sweated labor.

When a country receives goods of the same sort it is producing it may well ask: "Have these goods been subsidized? Are they being sold here at lower prices than in the country they came from? Is labor in that country being exploited, or being paid wages less than the standard in that country, in order to force these goods on the world market?"

There are many products, however, which can move in international trade without being open to such criticisms. Many countries can produce certain goods for export because of superior natural advantages and superior technical skill and at the same time pay wages to labor in keeping with the wage scale of the country. Such products, when they move in international trade, furnish real advantages to the countries that import them. Even when the country importing them may be able to produce the same products, a certain amount of imports may serve as a check on unfair monopoly prices in the receiving country. There should be more rather than less of this kind of international trade. Consumers in the United States deserve better protection in some instances from companies which use the tariff to support inflated capital structures and excessive prices. Moderate competition from abroad in these cases would work toward the general good.

We need to keep clearly in mind the difference between accepting subsidized or unfairly produced import products and accepting imports that can be honestly offered us because of natural advantages in the producing countries.

Nations throughout the world, however, are not only refusing to accept imports which they might advantageously receive, even though they produce the same products, but in many cases they are refusing to accept dissimilar products and going to great expense to produce these products in their own countries. They are pursuing such a policy because of the strange but intense desire of nations under highly developed capitalism to sell as much as possible and to buy as little as possible.

This theory, widespread as it is, is altogether absurd. Obviously if any nation were to export all that it produces and import nothing it would soon starve to death. It should be just as obvious that to export continually twice as much as a country imports means in the long run that the country is losing an amount of wealth equal to the difference between the goods sent out and the goods taken in. For in the long run, foreign nations must default on payments for goods they take, to the extent that they cannot send back goods in exchange.

There must be some reason for this persistent desire of modern nations to sell more than they buy. In the case of debtor nations the reason is not far to seek. Debtor nations must try to balance their

books by sending goods out of the country to pay
off principal and interest on their debts. In the case of
creditor nations, like the United States, this reason
does not hold, and there must be other reasons.

One reason, of course, is that the push behind each
export commodity is the push of the group primarily
interested in that one commodity; immediate self-
interest blinds the group to the welfare of the nation
as a whole. Similarly, the insistence on keeping out
each import commodity is the insistence of the group
primarily interested in the domestic production of
that commodity. Again the immediate self-interest
of a single group excludes consideration of the general
welfare.

We will not get very far in the solution of our international trade problem if our policies as a nation
are to be dictated by the demands of these separate
pressure groups of selfish producers. There is only
one way to formulate wise national policies, and
that is in the light of their effect on the nation as a
whole. The people of a nation, while they are made
up of separate groups of producers with separated
producing interests, also make up one large body of
consumers, and as consumers their interests are
identical. They want more and better goods to consume. The only way to see whether a policy works
out well or not is to see whether it gives more or less
of the right kind of goods for people as a whole to
consume.

From this point of view, the madness of wanting

to ship out of the country as much of its produced wealth as possible and to take in as little as possible of the produced wealth of other countries is at once evident. But to recognize this as madness is not to do away with it. Nations are still influenced much more by producer psychology than by consumer psychology. Producers everywhere over the world were led into a trap by the demands of the World War and were financially slaughtered after the war by the combination of falling prices, over-expansion, high taxes, burdensome debt and the rest. When prices fall producer groups become increasingly powerful politically, and during the 1920's and early 1930's producers were trying to put across programs through every government of the world that would salvage their assets in a period of deflation.

The influence of producers in national policies was probably at a peak in 1933. From now on, in so far as prices rise throughout the world, it may be expected that producers will be somewhat less interested in obtaining special benefits from governments, and excessive restrictions on international trade will relax. The possibility of another war is the one thing most likely to interfere with the gradual manifestation of this trend beginning in the near future.

The great need in the next few years will be to recover a sane idea of the advantages of the right kind of international trade. This is no great problem when two nations have utterly dissimilar products, such as rubber and wheat, to exchange. The problem

comes when nations have somewhat similar products
to exchange, and are unwilling to recognize mutual
advantages in price or in specific utility. Formerly it
was possible for Great Britain to send certain kinds
of textiles to Germany, while Germany sent certain
kinds of textiles to Great Britain; and for the United
States to export certain types of automobiles to
Europe and to import other types from there. In this
way a modest exchange of goods and services could
be maintained, despite the tendency of the countries
concerned to become more alike in their industrial
structure.

To make this policy work, however, will mean that
the people who need additional goods within the
country must have the means to buy those goods.
One of the reasons why nations try so hard to export
surplus products is that the people within the country who have the income to buy at least part of these
products are already supplied, while those who need
them lack the buying power. Surplus producing
groups thus go to all lengths to open up markets
abroad, instead of devising ways of increasing consumption among low-income groups at home. At
the same time, other producing groups, anxious to
keep as much as possible of the limited domestic
market to themselves, seek to raise tariffs in order
to keep out competing foreign products which they
themselves can produce, though at a higher cost.
The result, as we have noted before, is less of either
foreign or domestically produced goods to distribute
within the country and at higher prices.

Thus the foreign trade problem is domestic as well as international. Its solution requires in part an increase in domestic consumption. In other words, the pressure of exportable surpluses would not be so great if we had a better distribution of income so that the people who want goods will have the means of buying them. We need to think less about so-called favorable balances of trade and more about making goods available to people, whether produced at home or abroad, for the only real material wealth is desirable goods, not money or notes.

We need to think about the fact that our imports now are less than 4 percent of the value of our domestic production, when under normal world trade conditions we would be importing around 7 percent, or 75 percent more. This would mean an increase in imports of perhaps a billion to a billion and a half dollars, but since over the years a dollar of imports means also a dollar of exports, our exports would increase by about the same amount. A removal of foreign trade barriers would thus mean a general increase in industrial activity. Increased exports and increased industrial activity would supply the consumer purchasing power to absorb the increased imports.

As a matter of fact, imports in themselves create a substantial amount of domestic employment and purchasing power in their handling at the docks, their re-shipment, wholesaling and retailing before they finally reach the consumer. When this employment directly created by imports is added to the

employment imports bring about through supporting a roughly similar amount of exports, it becomes plain that the nation has very little to lose
and a great deal to gain by furthering two-way trade
with foreign countries.

These considerations should make all of us think
very carefully before we advocate measures which
are likely to impede rather than advance two-way
trade. Farmers particularly should be wary of policies which might result in further loss of mutual
trade. While at first glance they might believe it a
good thing if all competitive farm exports were ex-
cluded, they should realize that for every bushel or
pound of foreign stuff that might be kept off the
domestic market by an exclusionist policy, there are
some four or five bushels or pounds of stuff produced on our own surplus export acres which are
waiting and ready to be dumped on the home market.

The same considerations should make us all wary
of a policy that would attempt to force our foreign
trade in the one direction of exports without providing for a return of imports. While such a policy
might work for a given product for a short time, if
pursued generally and with no control of production
at home, it would result first in our giving away a
share of our wealth and soil-fertility to foreign nations, second in retaliations from abroad that would
actually make our export trade more difficult, and
finally in the collapse of the policy through domestic
overproduction and increasingly costly subsidies.

The sensible thing to do, then, is to seek to improve our consuming power for goods, both by measures which may distribute purchasing power more effectively at home, and by an intelligent fostering of two-way trade so that activities both in selling to and buying from foreign countries will increase.

Certainly there is no relief to be had through one-way trade. When every country tries at the same time to develop "favorable" balances of trade by means of export subsidies and import restrictions the result is paralysis for all. That sort of unbalanced trade, with its necessary dependence on foreign loans, colonies, concessions, and offensive international economic policies simply piles up grief to come, the least of which is defaulted payments and the more ominous of which is the flaming cataclysm of international war. It may be true that as nations come of age industrially they tend to have less that can usefully be exchanged. But it is also true that more highly developed nations increase the variety of their needs, and they should at the same time increase their capacity to consume. It is wise to develop all the possibilities of increased trade, both at home and with other countries, for the two alternatives are complete self-containment or aggressive imperialism, and both are bad.

Chapter XI

MACHINERY AND THE GENERAL WELFARE

WHETHER technology and machinery can be made the servants of man rather than harsh taskmasters is going to have a great deal to do with the general welfare of the United States in the decades ahead of us.

Previous to 1914 the belief in Progress Unlimited via the machine route was almost universal. In the '20s the faith was re-established among the upper classes of the great cities of the United States. Faith in progress and new inventions had become the real religion of most of the well-to-do citizens. It is small wonder that this should have been so. For more than a century new inventions have increased the power at the disposal of the average citizen. Every decade of that century had brought new peaks in industrial activity and new peaks in invention.

In the machine age of 1929 the average person in the United States had at his disposal ten times the horsepower at the disposal of the average person in 1787, and probably forty times as much if automotive power is included. Inventions had made it possible for succeeding generations of those men who were employed to get higher wages for greater productivity, work shorter hours and enjoy more of leisure and the good things of life. The economies of these inventions were in time passed on to consumers and contributed to the general welfare. Those workers who were displaced somehow found their way into the new frontiers or into new occupations that were springing up around the ever-growing industrial centers.

But after 1910 and particularly during the '20s unemployment began more and more to appear. Labor organized more vigorously to combat it, to raise wages and to lower the number of hours of work a week—all of which seemed to result in a greater premium than ever on inventions. Machines were devised during the late '20s and early '30s which in many lines enabled one man to do the work of ten, twenty, thirty or even a hundred.

It is true that from the beginning of the industrial revolution, workers and other persons made dire predictions concerning the tyranny of the machine over human beings. In England workers smashed new machinery which they feared would eliminate their jobs; Mary Godwin Shelley in 1818 symbolically portrayed the horrible triumph of mechanism over life in *Frankenstein*; and in the United States, in 1887, Labor Commissioner Wright wrote a pessimistic report which not only cited technology as an important factor in depressions, but prophesied that the day of great expansion of industry was over. He wrote:

This full supply of economic tools to meet the wants of nearly all branches of commerce and industry is the most important factor in the present industrial depression. It is true that the discovery of new processes of manufacture will undoubtedly continue, and this will act as an ameliorating influence, but it will not leave room for a marked extension, such as has been witnessed during the last fifty years, or afford a remunerative employment of the vast amount of capital which has been created during that period. The market price of products will continue low, no matter what the cost of production may be. The day of large profits is probably past. There may be room for further intensive, but not extensive, development of industry in the present area of civilization.

But as long as there was free or cheap unoccupied land of good quality and as long as the stream of inventions opened up new industries and occupations as fast as machinery displaced workers in old ones, the dire predictions never held true for long. There might be a temporary lag between displacement and re-employment, but always industry went on to new heights of activity, employment recovered and the general standard of living rose. New wheat and cotton lands were opened in the last quarter of the nineteenth century; in the 1890's we extended our railroads; the automobile industry sprang up rapidly after 1900; we created new opportunities for ourselves and millions of immigrants in steel, rubber, oil, cement and other industries; the World War speeded up activities of all sorts; we produced twice as much for Europe as we used to; between 1919 and

1929 we added 50 percent more power and 40 percent more productivity per wage earner; and not until the nationwide speculative spree of 1928–29 had collapsed did the old warnings and predictions seem serious again.

A century and a half of mechanical progress has brought us now, in a decade of restricted foreign markets and inadequate domestic purchasing power, squarely against the problem of technological unemployment in the cities and technologically induced low standards of living on our farms. The economies of inventions are not being so freely passed on to the consumer or passed back to workers in the form of higher wages and shorter hours; profits to the few have outrun wages and purchasing power to many. Whatever the past or future contributions of machines to the general welfare, we cannot turn our backs on a technological problem which between 1929 and 1936 had apparently resulted in the displacement of some millions of workers who may not expect re-employment even if the production level of 1929 is regained.

The machines of 1787 were quite respectful of State lines. Few people traveled across State lines and most goods were consumed within a few miles of where they were produced. It often took several weeks for news to travel completely over the entire United States. Some people marvel at the difficulty of governing a country the size of the United States and quote a saying attributed to Aristotle that no political unit should be larger than can be reached by one man's voice. In answer to Aristotle we might say that by means of the radio it is possible for one man to reach sixty million people instantly and by means of the sound movie for one man to be seen and heard by seventy-five million within two weeks. As long as the policy of those in control of the radio, the movie and the newspaper is not infected by principles contrary to the general welfare, and the public is given unbiased facts upon which to form its opinion, it would seem to be possible for a country the size of the United States in 1936 to be governed with even greater efficiency than the United States of 1787. In such a case, however, it may be necessary to think clearly and directly about the problems imposed by machinery operating on a continent-wide scale without the confusion which finds its origin in precedents growing out of the early days of the United States when use of machinery was limited and local in nature and did not have a continent-wide significance.

The technology and machinery of the past are the merest prelude to what we may expect in the future in case mankind continues to worship mechanized progress as the supreme god. In every type of production, whether agricultural or industrial, there are methods which are either now well-known or which can easily be brought within our grasp within a few years, the total effect of which would be to double production, or throw half of the employed onto the

streets unless we see to it that the increased efficiency
is fully shared with the workers involved or unless
displaced workers are definitely given new opportunities to maintain their standard of living.

Technological advances in agriculture have a somewhat different bearing on the general welfare than
do similar advances in other lines of production.
Increases in industrial efficiency have in the past
brought increased volume, lower prices, increased
wages and, for displaced workers, jobs in new occupations. Increases in agricultural efficiency have also
redounded to the benefit of consumers, but here the
natural limit to domestic consumption determined
by the constant per capita requirements has forced
farm population into non-farm occupations rather
than into increasing the total production of farm
products. During the past thirty years, 1900 to 1930,
for example, we had about the same total population
on farms—around 30 million. The excess of births
over deaths has gone to help expand the non-farm
population from about 46.5 million in 1900 to about
92 million in 1930. The total population increased
about 60 percent while the farm population remained
stationary.

During this period the per capita consumption
of farm products remained practically unchanged,
as it had in previous generations. Between 1900 and
1930, a stationary number of people on farms produced enough food and basic clothing materials for
a demand that increased 60 percent. In other words

agriculture had increased its efficiency by about 60 percent in 30 years and it could probably do it again during the next 30 years.

The industrial depression has made agriculture at least 10 percent less efficient since 1930 for it not only checked the flow of excess farm population to industrial centers but actually unloaded several million people in farm communities. We now have nearly 33 million people on farms producing food and clothing for a total population of 127 million people where less than 30 million could do the necessary work.

If a great corporation were running the agriculture of the United States, it would be possible within ten years, by the use of suitable rotations, the application of lime and fertilizer, the planting of improved varieties, the use of new types of machinery, the employment of more efficient types of livestock and the feeding of better balanced rations, to produce the present agricultural output with only a little over half as much labor. The present quantity of livestock products in the corn belt could be produced with thirty million acres of corn instead of fifty million acres. Of course, under individualistic methods the progress will not be as rapid, but at the present rate of advance in agricultural technique, it is safe to anticipate that within twenty years the necessary farm products in the United States can be produced with at least 20 percent fewer people living on the land than in 1936.

Industry is younger than agriculture and the potentialities of improving efficiency are theoretically much greater. A new type of power production like electricity increased a hundred-fold during the thirty-one years from 1897 to 1928. During the same time both agricultural production and population in the United States increased only about 60 percent. Newcomers such as electric power, the radio, the movie, the automobile and the airplane have for a time grown at a speed one hundred or even two hundred times as fast as agriculture. These rapidly expanding industries all functioning together at their time of greatest growth can absorb the displaced labor and most of the increased output resulting from improved agricultural efficiency. But when they lose their youth, when no new rapidly expanding industries are coming along, and the millions of city workers remain unemployed, the problem of a balanced relationship between agriculture and industry becomes one of very great significance.

It is not generally realized that mechanization in agriculture making for increased production at lower unit costs can not be materially offset by increased consumption. If wheat production costs were cut in two it would lower the price of a loaf of bread by about half a cent, and a nation that consumes five bushels of wheat per capita irrespective of price, and irrespective of prosperity or depression, will not consume additional low cost production except through developing new uses. But if these new uses merely substitute wheat for other products, the advantage to wheat growers becomes a disadvantage to other producers of foods. This is a basic limitation to all non-liquid food consumption. All food products compete for their share in a fairly rigid per capita budget and any increased preference given to wheat, or pork or beans is at the expense of some other item in the food budget. The national stomach is not as extensible as is the national capacity to utilize an ever expanding list of industrial goods and services.

It is true that consumption of farm products could be increased somewhat and farm activity increased considerably if the families who now are poorly fed and clothed could obtain the purchasing power to buy more and better food and clothing. Particularly, if low-income groups were able to shift from poor-grade diets made up of an excessive proportion of cereals to higher-grade diets including larger proportions of vegetables, milk, fruits and meat of good quality, more farm acreage would be needed and more hours of farm work. This desirable shift, however, could be brought about only by a better distribution of income among consumers than now exists, so that those with inadequate incomes at present would be able to pay farmers the increased price required by higher-grade foods.

As long as the domestic demand for farm products remains inelastic and foreign trade restricted, further major advances in the mechanization of agriculture can mean only one thing, and that is the release of farm labor; and the released labor can have but two avenues of escape—one is into non-farm private employment, the other is into socially created opportunities of work, education and leisure. It can of course also remain in the farm community to share a limited and probably reduced return from more efficient production. It is this dilemma that the South is now fearful of as the day of the mechanical cotton picker approaches with its certain release of farm labor that will have no place to go to.

Since 1932 it has been amazing to see how much more we can produce without materially reducing the number of the unemployed. In the early part of 1933 factory production and factory employment had fallen to only 60 percent of what it had been 10 years earlier. Within a span of four months under the drive of prospective New Deal changes employment was increased about 20 percent and hours about 10 percent but production was increased 67 percent. On the average every employed worker in 1933 was about 27 percent more productive than in 1929. Naturally the pace in the summer of 1933 could not be maintained for long for it meant a great deal of unbalanced activity, too much of some goods and not enough of others.

The average factory worker can now turn out about 30 percent more than he did seven years ago. We could now produce the 1929 volume of industrial

goods with considerably less factory employees than
in 1929, but the improved efficiency would not be
all clear gain because all of us have to support
directly or indirectly the workers whom the increased efficiency displaces.

The time is undoubtedly overdue for the American
people to become enormously enthusiastic about
something more than new inventions and technology. New machinery, efficient workers and integrated methods of production are not enough in
either agriculture or industry. The whole industrial
machine must balance, and there must be no serious
unemployment of those who really want to work
and who have at least a moderate capacity to work.

The industrial unemployment problem, like the
agricultural difficulty, is not a local matter. It is
nation-wide in its nature and demands national co-
ordination of agricultural and industrial policies in
line with the postwar creditor position of the United
States.

In the summer of 1935, 13 percent of the population, a total of 16 million persons received emergency
relief. These people on relief were located in every
State. The wheat States suffering from their inability to sell the usual 20 percent of their wheat
production abroad, the live stock producing States
suffering from the lack of purchasing power in the
industrial centers, the industrial States suffering
from the inability of industry in general to utilize
its productive capacity for turning out more goods

for more people in need of them—all were weighed
down by these common interrelated problems of
reduced foreign trade, unemployment, and machine
power not used to its full potentialities for abundant
goods, more general consumption and more leisure
for cultural pursuits.

There is some reason to believe that the fanat-
ically religious worship of the machine and the technique surrounding it which characterized the nineteenth and early twentieth centuries will begin to
pass in the not very distant future. Perhaps for
another fifteen or twenty years the machine and the
efficiency methods which accompany it will be
exalted above social values and the qualities of
enjoyment, understanding and appreciation which
flow from a knowledge of life as contrasted with the
competitive drive of the machine. Part of the havoc
worked by the machine, I believe, has grown out
of an ill-proportioned philosophy of life. The United
States more than any other nation except Russia
has committed its inmost spirit to the discipline of
the machine, but the younger generation is now
asking, more than ever before: "What is it all about?
What is worth while?" There is a growing interest
in the biological sciences, in wild life, in the appreciation of nature and of life in the open air. Workers
in the cities are gradually becoming interested in the
so-called satellite cities where there is more air and
sunshine and some ground for a garden. Gradually
humanity in the United States is beginning to think

in terms of co-operative life and enjoyment and not merely in terms of competition in money, power, profit and machinery.

While it is possible that the 1936 model of the New Deal will not be completely successful, it is almost certain that the American people will not long tolerate the dominance of their lives by machine technology. They are determined to make the machine their servant. They do not propose to see it go up and down the land much longer increasing unemployment. They want to see such balanced use of the machine technology that all of us can have more of the good things of life, that all of us can have more leisure to enjoy such simple things as fresh air and sunshine without thereby endangering the security of our job or the security of our old age. If we are worthy of the name of men we can in time force the machine to give us these things.

Chapter XII

CORPORATIONS AND THE GENERAL WELFARE

MORE than any other single factor, the use made of the corporate form of organization is going to determine the economic welfare of the United States in the years directly ahead. If we can learn how to use this tremendous instrument of business to build consumption as efficiently as it now can build production, the general welfare may reach unheard-of high levels. If we can't learn how to use the corporate form to promote consumption continuously on a truly broad scale, we may well slide into another pit of depression worse than the last.

It has become the fashion to approach this question of corporations and the general welfare by dwelling on the abuses of corporate power, after the age-old custom of seeking for personal devils. Corporations are pictured as ruthless monsters, urged on in their nefarious work by small, interlocking groups of directors who are no better than conspirators against the public, but accountable in the last analysis to no one, and which grow larger with every effort to curb them. This approach is gratifying to the sense of moral indignation, but for my own part I think it will get us nowhere.

It is true that some corporations have abused their powers and pursued their ends in underhanded ways. Some have practically owned public officials and used them to secure preferential legislation. Many have played a game of hide and seek between State and Federal authorities, championing States' rights at one time and unified Federal power at another, according to the expediency of the moment. Some have employed shrewd legal counsel solely to out-trick or out-wit all opposition. A few have tried to buy and control newspapers, or otherwise secretly to influence public opinion. In a few extreme instances, corporate directors have deliberately wrecked concerns entrusted to their management in order to line their pockets with the investments of duped and ruined stockholders.

But it is not fair to generalize from exceptional cases, however hideous they may be. Most corporations have been guilty of nothing more sinister than using the powers and laws available to them to build up their industries successfully against competition and make profits for their management and stockholders.

No, this chapter is not going to deal with abuses of corporate power, but with the relation of the corporation as such to the general welfare, and with some of the changes which corporate business may have to undergo if it is to survive and make as worthy a contribution to the America of tomorrow as it made to the America of yesterday. Even if it were possible to remove over night all the abuses of centralized economic power that have been practiced by corporations, the fundamental problem involved in the relation of the corporation to the general welfare would remain unsolved. This problem has to do with the corporate structure as such, with its capacity to provide our people with work at adequate wages, to build purchasing power as well as profits, to promote consumption as well as production.

In 1787 corporations meant practically nothing to the general welfare of the United States. Our Constitution was written for a people who transacted 99 percent of their business through individuals and partnerships. Even by 1870 corporations had no great country-wide significance, although enterprising men were beginning to discover the usefulness of the corporate form of organization and some few were preparing to profit by it in a most extraordinary fashion. Farmers here and there became alarmed and in some instances began to fight the "trusts" in the different States with anti-monopoly legislation.

As early as 1869, for example, a group of farmers met in Bloomington, Illinois, and declared that, "nothing can be accomplished for the enforcement of our rights, and the redress of our wrongs, without an efficient organization on the well-known principles that give the great corporations such tremendous power." Labor made a similar struggle for

equality through the labor union. No one in 1870,
however, could possibly have guessed the tremendous triumph that was coming to the corporate form
of business organization during the next sixty years.

And yet today more than 95 percent of those who
work in our mines, our factories, on our railroads,
and for our public utilities are working for corporations. Great corporations tend to concentrate and
consolidate their gains during a depression. From
1929 to 1932 the 200 largest non-financial corporations increased their share of non-financial corporate
assets from 49 percent to 56 percent of the total.
If the rate at which the 200 largest corporations
have been growing since 1909 is maintained in the
future they will control 70 percent of our corporate
wealth by 1950.

The struggle against the growing power of corporations which was made before the turn of the
century has been largely forgotten. Corporate charters were granted at first only to limited types of
industry and the life of corporations was restricted
to twenty, thirty, or, in exceptional cases, fifty years.
The New York State constitution at one time required a two-thirds vote of both houses before a
charter could be granted, while other States went so
far as to demand ratification by popular vote where
banking powers were concerned. Limitations upon
the amount of authorized capital were the custom
for many years. As late as 1881 the maximum for
general business corporations in New York was two

million dollars, and until 1890, five million. The less industrialized States had much smaller capital stock limitations, and were reluctant to relinquish them, while Texas still has a limit for certain corporations. Pennsylvania did not remove the restriction as to size until 1905, and New Hampshire waited until 1919. In general, however, we passed from an age of Corporations Limited at the end of the nineteenth century and entered an era of Corporations Unlimited with the beginning of the twentieth century.

As late as 1909, the small business man was still dominant in the field of retailing, but the general tide swept on and by 1919 the number of chain stores doubled, then trebled, and by 1930 more than half of retailing was corporate. All fields of business activity seem to be coming under the sway of the corporation, although farming still remains largely an exception. At least 95 percent of the output of agriculture is by individuals,* whereas only a small fraction of our manufacturing output is by small business men who are still outside the corporate set-up. No wonder some critics are alarmed. They point to the triumph of the state over the church in the medieval struggle for temporal power, and

---

* The Triple-A checks made out to large corporations indicate that sugar cane production is largely under the control of corporations but that most other agriculture is still being conducted for the most part by family-sized units. While more than 95 percent of the farms are individualistic enterprises, it must be remembered that nearly half of these farms are run by tenants and of the remainder nearly half are heavily mortgaged.

remind us that two opposing masters cannot sit together in the seats of the mighty. Some of them carry the analogy one step further and predict that the corporation is about to swallow up the state.

The corporation had the soundest reasons for coming into being. It started as a venture in co-operation. It enabled men to pool their money, and in that way to carry out a venture which was beyond the means of any one man, however rich he might be. Previously-scattered individuals took their first kindergarten lessons in team play, and one giant enterprise after another came into being. The canal, the railroad and the telegraph spread through a broad land and promised to bring Americans together into one big family. Invention followed invention, and the promised land of abundance came within range—a new era was actually being born before the very eyes of those who had engineered the first crude starts. Captains of industry became the idols of the younger generation, and America was untroubled by the warning of any powerful Jeremiah. Corporations fought for increased power, and the States fought each other in one mad scramble to grant such power freely. Delaware finally emerged victorious, and the home of the softest corporate charters became the legal residence of our most hard-headed industries.

America was moving rapidly away from the days of the Founding Fathers. Certainly they never intended that Delaware, through her State laws, should name the conditions under which business was to be done in all the other States of the Union, whether they like them or not. Nor could anyone have foreseen in 1870 that within sixty years there would be a hundred ragged individuals at the bottom for every rugged one at the top. Perhaps it was better so; young America had a job to do, and in many ways it was done amazingly well. In half a century we had colonized a continent and raised the standard of living enormously by learning how to make useful things efficiently.

The corporate form of organization must be given much of the credit for the speed with which all this was accomplished. As a means of rapidly establishing the machinery of production in virgin country there is certainly no parallel for it in all history. The corporation is the most efficient instrument of production yet devised. Can we say as much for it as an instrument for promoting consumption? For a while it looked as though we could.

The investment of surplus profits in additional machinery to make more things for more people not only kept our workers employed but up to 1929 it looked very much like an open road to an ultimate economy of abundance for our whole people. In the years just before the crash, however, profits which once went into new homes and new factories were actively misused to promote speculation, while in the depression which followed much of this surplus money was not used at all. Faced with this cruel

paradox of idle men and idle dollars, it was inevitable that men should challenge the corporation as an
instrument for promoting consumption.

The American system of private ownership cannot
go on if we are going to continue to concentrate
power and wealth in the hands of fewer and fewer
men. We have gone dangerously far as it is in denying the mass of people any real property stake in the
country. Early in our history nearly all of our people
owned their own homes. Today more than half of
our people live in rented homes. For those who rent
as well as for many of those who own their homes,
shelter and security depend on the continuation of
their jobs. These people never know when some
"change in the business cycle" or some "order from
the home office" will deprive them of their jobs
even though they are doing their work efficiently.
The power to start and stop a plant at will is relatively harmless in the hands of the small business
man, but to give this same right to our huge impersonal corporations which employ millions of
people is quite another matter. The time has certainly come to set up some social safeguards; there
is enough dynamite in the exercise of this power to
wreck our whole economic structure, including the
corporations themselves.

Between the peak of the 1929 boom and the bottom of the depression, industrial production as a
whole fell off nearly half and some of the more
highly centralized corporations cut their output by

eighty percent. Millions of competent workers were "plowed out" into the streets, and those who remained in their jobs at reduced wages felt disposed to thank God for having escaped actual starvation. Even a corporation with the high reputation of the American Telephone and Telegraph Company felt obliged under the rules of the game to reduce the number of its employees by 32 percent and its payrolls by 26 percent between 1929 and 1935, while its revenues fell only 13 percent and while it maintained dividends undiminished. Under the rules of the game when volume falls off, a continuous dividend policy takes precedence over a continuous employment policy. Since 1932, the Government has dealt with some of the more acute phases of the emergency which private business was not able or willing to deal with. The Social Security Act is an effort to meet in advance some of the worst effects of the next depression. But the central problems of shaping an industrial system which can prevent depressions remain to be solved.

We may well question whether the "corporation" (this strange figure of speech that means a person that isn't a person) has the right to all those legal liberties and freedom from surveillance which actual persons should and do have under our American form of government. When corporations acquire the benefits of great accumulations of capital and of co-operative skill, when their operations take on nation-wide scope and involve the security of millions of people, we may well ask whether they have not foregone their privileges as "persons" and taken on some of the responsibilities of public institutions. Certainly the framers of the Constitution never fore-saw that the clauses protecting a "person's" right to "life, liberty and property" would be invoked to protect the privileges and often to avoid the respon-sibilities of impersonal and immortal billion-dollar corporations. We may well consider whether our laws should not recognize the distinction.

The concentration of economic power in our great corporations has deprived the individual of any chance to bargain with them on an equal footing. The small unorganized stockholders have no real voice at a board of directors' meeting. The laborer who goes to work past a line of men applying for jobs at the same plant feels the weakness of his position. The white-collared employee who works for a corporation which he knows has an informal agree-ment with its competitors not to hire each other's men thinks twice before he asks for a raise or resigns his job. The farmer is equally helpless; as one of several million he sells his produce at "the market" to the few corporations which buy from him, and as a consumer of city goods he is obliged to buy on a "take it or leave it" basis. The consumer who doesn't like the way in which he is treated by some electric light company can either make the best of it or go back to lamps. This does not mean that the individual is always right and the corporation always wrong, but it does mean that the individual is no match for the huge corporate enterprise. He has about as much chance as if he were dealing with a regiment single-handed. Capitalism was built upon the principle of free and fair competition between free and evenly matched men, but this has become a farce in the face of monopolies. No individual can hold his own against a billion-dollar corporation.

I realize the gravity of the practical problems which face our business men and sympathize with them in their difficulties. I know that as trustees of invested capital they are often forced to adopt wage, employment, price and production policies that do not square with the general welfare. Unfortunately that does not remove the problems. The brutal truth is that industry must rise above its primary obligation to invested capital or face the danger of being torn loose from its moorings in the next major depression. Capitalism must either learn to promote consumption in the same magnificent fashion in which it has built our national productive plant, or capitalism will eventually perish. When a mere fraction of our people worked for corporations, it was only natural that their managers should escape any popular demand that they conduct their affairs in the interest of the general welfare. Now that they employ a majority of our workers there is a reasonable and growing demand that they shoulder their social responsibilities. Millions of Americans are convinced that corporations must either adjust themselves to provide jobs for those who want work or give way to some alternative structure which will. Obviously business cannot continue to turn its back on a problem like that of unemployment without sooner or later being stabbed in the back.

When business men are told: "You must provide jobs for the unemployed," the business man answers, "I'd be glad to if I could. But I can't take on more men unless there is a greater demand for goods. I am not operating a charitable institution. I can't increase my payroll if it means producing at a loss." When it is said in reply: "Increase employment and payrolls, and the demand for more goods will be created. Somebody has got to start the ball rolling," the business man has a ready answer. "If I try that by myself, I am only putting my head in a noose. My competitors will string me up. I will not only fail to provide new jobs, but destroy those I have provided, by going bankrupt."

The business man has the best of it when the argument stops at this point. The individual business man truly has very limited scope for tackling the problem single-handed. But unfortunately, though he is right with the situation as it is, the problem remains. If solving it means changing the situation, the business man with the rest of us must help make the change or we will all go down together.

The air is filled with many conflicting answers to this more fundamental question. "Let us alone," the tories still insist, while the radicals assert, "Produce for use." Many who take the middle of the road are honestly searching for ways to make our system of private ownership work. The effort is a genuine one to save corporate business from its own excesses so that the principles of democracy and liberty may be perpetuated. One such group believes that bigness as such should be smashed, and that if there is any ensuing chaos it will be a cheap price to pay for having escaped State Fascism. These men honestly feel that we should return to the days of our earlier history and build the country on the little business man, with such encouragement for consumer-co-operatives as local conditions seem to warrant. Two of the justices of the Supreme Court have spoken very forcefully on this matter in their recent dis-senting opinions in the case of Ligget vs. Lee. Justice Brandeis said in part:

The prevalence of the corporation in America has led men of this generation to act, at times, as if the privilege of doing business in corporate form were inherent in the citizen; and has led them to accept the evils attendant upon the free and unrestricted use of the corporate mechanism as if these evils were the inescapable price of civilized life and, hence, to be borne with resignation. Throughout the greater part of our history a different view prevailed. Although the value of this instrumentality in commerce and industry was fully recognized, incorporation for business was commonly denied long after it had been freely granted for religious, educational and charitable purposes. It was denied because of fear. Fear of encroachment upon the liberties and opportunities of the individual. Fear of the subjection of labor to capital. Fear of monopoly. Fear that the absorption of capital by corporations, and their perpetual life, might bring evils similar to those which attended mortmain. There was a sense of some insidious menace inherent in large aggregations of capital, particularly when held by corporations.

Speaking in much the same vein, Justice Cardozo said:

There is a widespread belief that the existing unemployment is the result, in large part, of the gross inequality in the distribution of wealth and income which giant corporations have fostered; that by the control which the few have exerted through giant corporations, individual initiative and effort are being paralyzed, creative power impaired and human happiness lessened; that the true prosperity of our past came not from big business, but through the courage, the energy and the resourcefulness of small men; that only by releasing from corporate control the faculties of the unknown many, only by reopening to them the opportunities for leadership, can confidence in our future be restored and the existing misery be overcome; and that only through participation by the many in the responsibilities and determinations of business, can Americans secure the moral and intellectual development which is essential to the maintenance of liberty.

Another group, however, sees no harm in bigness as such. Rather it would seek to retain the advantages of bigness, but find ways of directing such advantages to a broader public interest and of eliminating the misuses of power that develop when bigness is unregulated. One suggestion of those who think along this line is that all corporations whose business overlaps State boundaries be licensed under a system of Federal charters.

Such a system, many believe, would make it possible to deal with some of the problems which States have been utterly unable to deal with under a system of State charters for interstate corporations. Leading States which refuse to relax their corporate laws have been left out in the cold by industrialists seeking to escape regulation. Lesser States, eager for the revenue to be derived from traffic in corporate charters, have not only written laws according to the blueprints of business men, but have advertised their willingness to do so. Thus in 1901, the Secretary of State of Delaware advertised: "It is believed that no State has on its statute books more complete and liberal laws than these," and the advantages to business men seeking charters were then enumerated.

Faced with such competition, other States have been helpless to maintain any high standards for business incorporation. Woodrow Wilson tried to reform the corporate laws of New Jersey, but his reforms were quickly undone by legal repeal in 1917. One State after another has had to capitulate to lax corporation laws to keep their industries from migrating to more friendly climates for corporations. A situation in which a corporation can secure its Delaware charter and have its name printed on an

office door in the Corporation Trust Company building of Wilmington and then invade if it wants to
every other State in the Union under conditions
definitely to the disadvantage of local businesses is a
situation that offends the national sense of fair play.

Thus the proposal to require Federal charters for
interstate corporations would seem to be a minimum
step toward bringing bigness more in line with the
general welfare. It is a mechanism that may well
help to assure protection for investors and at the
same time secure socially adequate standards of
wages and working conditions for labor in these
great industries. Its advocates believe it may provide a method for increasing and stabilizing consumer purchasing power and thereby assure an
adequate market for our business men and our
farmers.

At the core of the whole problem is the fundamental question: "Is the corporate form of organization, which has been so successful in the field of
production, sufficiently flexible to serve as a means
for increasing consumption?" If it is, there is no
height to which we cannot go; if it isn't, we are
going to pass through some dark days.

The corporate form of organization as it now
exists can be geared to greatly increased production
overnight, "if there is a demand," but there is no
similar device in the mechanism for increasing consumption. Forward-looking industrialists know that
one must be built if the machine is to keep on run-

ning. Already there are several half-drawn blueprints, calling for shorter hours, higher wages, lower
sales prices and dismissal grants of money to employees who have been thrown out of work by
improved machinery. All of these suggestions rest
on the fact that business as a whole practically controls its own market by fixing the salaries and wages
of its employees who, taken in the mass, are also
its customers. They also rest on the assumption
that one industry cannot do it alone, but that there
must be some plan for co-operation, by which businesses may together accomplish things which they
are helpless to accomplish separately.

The NRA was an effort to meet this need. In some
ways it was disappointing to its most ardent supporters, but it has great historic significance as our
first national effort to meet country-wide industrial
problems on a national scale. Conditions themselves
may force our various groups to undertake another
co-operative industrial program in the years just
ahead, in which event we can benefit greatly from
our first experience in this direction.

Any such co-operative plan, if it is to remain
democratic, must provide for real representation of
all the groups affected. These include labor and
representatives of the public interest as well as
capital and management. No single group can
safely be entrusted with the great responsibilities of
economic policies under complicated modern conditions. It seems to me that business men should wel-

come the sharing of such responsibilities in these
days when unsolved problems threaten the stability
of our society.

We need not be too impatient. The science of consumption no doubt has its own evolution to undergo,
and it is fully fifty years behind the science of production. But the time has certainly arrived to put
our energies and ingenuities to work on this new
science of consumption. From now on, the business
man who thinks only in terms of production and is
fatalistic toward the deeper problem of consumption
is a back number.

Those brilliant figures in modern business who
have made advertising a tremendous force in our
economic life should be the very people to turn their
attention from combing the possibilities of the available market to combing the possibilities of the
potential market that would be opened if the consumers who need goods and services had the means
to buy. Advertising men already know how many
Americans need new houses, new furniture, new
goods and services of all kinds. Some of them now
should study the underlying causes that prevent
business from tapping this great reserve market and
the means by which this market can be opened up.
If they succeed in such a task, they will make their
previous triumphs look small.

Young business men are therefore face to face with
the challenge of a lifetime. If they can match the
mechanism of production which they inherited from

their fathers with a comparable mechanism for increasing consumption, the next fifty years will be far more exciting than the last fifty. Like their fathers, however, they must cut new paths and not be halted by the criticism that it hasn't been done before. At the dawn of the machine age, men also said it hadn't been done before.

Reactionaries have fought every step of the way against the more enlightened practices of business, such as shortening hours, eliminating child labor, raising wages, reducing sales prices, and granting labor the right to collective bargaining. Such progress as we have made along these lines, however, has invariably worked out to the individual and the general good, and confounded reactionary critics. Undoubtedly business in the future must move deliberately in this direction, and to do so under modern conditions will mean some method of co-operative effort and co-operative planning. Today the individualist who refuses to think about and adopt the kind of social mechanisms which are needed to increase consumption is standing in the way of the future just as much as was the backward small business man fifty years ago who refused to adopt the mechanical devices or new forms of organization which were needed to increase production.

The empire builders and early captains of industry revealed imagination of a high order in mobilizing tools and capital to make productive the natural resources of the country. Our later financiers have too often been interested not in the application of new ideas to physical resources, but in tying up our economic empires in financial strait jackets which eliminate competition without distributing the benefits of monopoly, which solidify prices and profits at the expense of productivity. The leaders of the present and future must display imagination as daring as that of the early industrialists, but this imagination must deal with the co-operative machinery which can balance consumption with production on an ever-broadening scale.

Getting our huge production machine geared to the needs of consumption will not be accomplished without a good deal of struggle and grief. Some people's toes will be stepped on. All kinds of smoke screens will be raised, from "government interference" to Bolshevism. I think American common sense can be trusted to keep calm in the face of such storms, just as I believe American ingenuity can be trusted to find our own kind of social mechanisms which are necessary to fulfill the promise of our wealth and good fortune. Not to risk the grief of this struggle for a revised economic machine is to invite the chaos sure to come if we ride along on the outdated old one. The essential thing is to fix our eyes steadfastly on the abundance within our grasp and be willing to take the hard first steps on the road to achieving it.

Part Three

WE THE PEOPLE

"Can it be supposed that this vast country including the Western territory will 150 years hence remain one nation?"
Statement in Constitutional Convention debate by Nathaniel Gorham of Massachusetts.

THE framers of the Constitution could never have foreseen, in their concrete modern forms, the problems of the fourth decade of the twentieth century which we have been discussing. Power machinery and modern technology, the corporate form of organization as now developed, an international picture with special twentieth century complications, changing trends in population, natural resources in process of serious depletion; the wisest man in 1787 could never have envisioned these problems in their present complexity. Yet the people of the United States living today have these problems to face. The next ten, twenty or thirty years are going to be crucial with respect to all or most of them. We who are going to live in this period will have to meet them in one way or another, and we are not going to have the benefit of face-to-face counsel with the wise men of 1787 in finding the way through.

What, then, of the political mechanism—the Constitution—which they bequeathed to us? Was it meant to exist for all time, and to be adaptable to conditions which they could not foresee? How has it been used and interpreted? What adaptations have been made, and have they been in line with living needs? What clues can be discovered as to the intent of the framers with respect to questions of granted powers, interpretation and adaptation according to living needs?

These questions are going to be extremely important ones to American people in the years directly ahead.

Chapter XIII

THE WISE YOUNG MEN OF 1787

THE Founding Fathers were young men who knew what they wanted, and were brilliantly successful in getting it.

Luther Martin, the Maryland delegate who quit the Constitutional Convention in anger, indignantly exclaimed that the Philadelphia assembly sought "a national, not a federal government." His remark was indiscreet, but true. The strong men of that convention were not gathered to doctor up the Articles of Confederation, or to devise another and equally weak compact between the States. They had had enough, in Washington's phrase, of such a rope of sand.

They sought a strong central government, a *national* government, and they got it. They sought national protection for private property, and they got it. They wished this power to extend as far as might be necessary to defend and nurture those economic interests which in their judgment comprised the General Welfare of 1787. They sought defense against enemies, foreign and domestic, and they knew that in union there is strength. In short, they sought all the grand objectives stated in the preamble to the Constitution, and they created within the body of the document the power to achieve them.

Only young men would have dared so much.* Only men who knew precisely what they wanted would have spent a long, hot summer in Philadelphia wrestling with the abstract means to a concrete end.

Consider the odds against them: State governments and State officials, however imperfect, were against any central government that might reduce any of their powers, and perquisites. Distance— magnificent distance in a machineless age—made the creation of a central government for four million widely scattered inhabitants seem all but hopeless. Colonial, local prejudices were prominent. Men would always, Madison feared, consider themselves citizens of Virginia, or New York, or Massachusetts, and only secondarily, if at all, citizens of the United States.

As if these odds were not great enough, there was an even greater obstacle to be feared in the sentiments and the behavior of the small farmers and the frontiersmen inland, and the mechanics and seaport workers along the coast. There was no telling what these people would do next. Their revolutionary zeal had not abated, though the Revolution was officially over in 1783. The phrases of the Decla-

* Madison, "Father of the Constitution," was only 36 in 1787, and Hamilton a mere 30. Charles Pinckney and others were under 30. The average age of the 55 delegates who attended the Convention was about 40.

ration of Independence continued to live in their hearts and minds. They had dethroned British rule and British aristocracy, not for the benefit of an American aristocracy of land and slaves and money, but for the benefit of the plain people. They welcomed the Revolution because they saw a chance to win a voice in government.

Their first opportunity to garner the fruits of victory came in the writing of State Constitutions. This was the golden opportunity to write their definition of democracy into imperishable law. They meant to end feudal land laws, and flat taxes on land and inequitable poll taxes. They would make it easier for a man to get western land to farm, and would throttle the speculators. Outside of New England they would abolish the State-subsidized church and the domination of the clergy. They wished justice to be convenient, and the seat of government to be central, not on the coast. And they would vastly extend the privilege of the ballot.

"Let the people rule!" they cried. So they pushed for powerful legislatures—but with the power subject to check by annual elections. As for the governor, make him a figurehead; and let the removal of judges be made easy.

Thus the impassioned believers in democracy, to the horror of most men of wealth and social position. A powerful legislature and a widespread ballot were not the prescription of the aristocrats of the day. They wished a careful balance of powers, subjecting

the legislature to restraint both by the other branches
of government and by the manner of its election—
by electors possessing certain property qualifications.
Leave the executive free to direct the administration, make the judiciary a bulwark of protection for
property, and the government would be dignified
and stable and in proper hands. A restricted ballot
was not an abuse, as they saw it, but a valuable
institution which recognized the inevitable economic
inequalities among men.

It is hard to say whether the conservatives or the
radical democrats won in the State Constitutions.
The theory of checks and balances was written into
most of these constitutions, but practice soon fell
short of theory. In Virginia, Jefferson—who even
then would have been thought a wild-eyed radical
in Connecticut—protested that all the power of
government was still concentrated in the legislature,
and "One hundred and seventy-three despots would
surely be as oppressive as one." On the other hand,
property qualifications for voting were still the rule
in eight of the thirteen States.* In terms of events

* Summarizing these early Constitutions, Allan Nevins, in *The American States During and After the Revolution, 1775–1789,* writes as
follows: "It is remarkable that of these first constitutions, four lasted
more than a half century: North Carolina's 75 years, New Jersey's 68,
Maryland's 65, and Virginia's 54. The Charter of Connecticut served as
a State Constitution for 42 years, and that of Rhode Island for no less
than 64. New York's Constitution, though mulled over by a convention
in 1801, endured substantially unaltered, its faults becoming ever more
flagrant, for 45 years. The others, including the temporary instrument of
Massachusetts, had comparatively brief careers, some being discarded

that took place under these State Constitutions up
to 1787, however, there was no doubt in the minds
of such men as Washington and Hamilton and Madison that the more ardent democrats had corralled
enough power to harass important economic interests.

The hard times of 1785–86 brought matters to a
head. Small farmers and tradesmen, heavily in debt,
were in some States shoving bills through the legislatures to the detriment of creditors. They were
clamoring for the States to issue bale upon bale of
paper money. In Massachusetts they were actually
arming themselves and attacking their creditors
and the courts, under the leadership of Daniel Shays.
This time they were suppressed, but whose property
could now be considered safe? Where would they

---

almost immediately—and not one too soon. .... Fortunately, the rapid
development of better State Constitutions was facilitated by the free
interchange of constitutional ideas, and the popular willingness of most
States to hold revising conventions. The obstacles to the calling of such
bodies were decidedly fewer than today. Outside the South, the vested
interests that might be injured by alterations were not so powerful as
they became within a few decades. Men were accustomed to the idea of
constitutional change, while most of the original instruments had been
adopted informally, and formalities took root only slowly. When later
the tide of constitutional revision ebbed, it was in part because a tendency had arisen to look upon the 'fathers' with peculiar reverence—a
tendency which Jefferson before his death deprecated. 'They ascribe to
men of the preceding age more wisdom than human, and suppose what
they did to be beyond improvement,' Jefferson complained. 'I know that
age well. I belonged to it and worked with it. .... It was very like the
present, but without the experience of the present, and 40 years experience in government is worth a century in book-reading.'"

break out next? And what if such a spirit of violence should spread southward, and infect the southern planters' slaves?

But it was what the hard times were doing to shipping and mercantile interests, and land speculation, and to owners of public as well as private paper, that precipitated action.

British Orders in Council had closed West Indian ports to all staples not carried in British bottoms, and French and Spanish restrictions were almost as bad. American shipping had no place to go.

British manufacturers dumped their surpluses on American shores. Infant American industries, built up during the Revolution, were smothering.

Merchants, even when they could find their way through a maze of fluctuating paper money and variegated coins, had still to figure on fluctuating State tariffs and retaliatory measures as between States.* And when the merchant's day's figuring was done, he all too frequently had to go to court to get his money, only to find it a court suspicious of any creditor living more than half a day's journey away.

Land values, particularly in the new territory to the west, declined for lack of a strong government to protect settlers against the Indians, and against the fears of British, French and Spanish invasion.

Perhaps worst of all, the value of public securities

* At one time New York levied duties on firewood from Connecticut and on cabbages from New Jersey.

was fast declining. Government paper was quoted at anywhere from one-sixth to one-twentieth of its face value. Interest on foreign obligations went unpaid, and on the domestic debt, arrears of interest doubled and quadrupled. The men who had financed the Revolution were not faring so well.

An impotent Congress, operating under the feeble Articles of Confederation, stood helplessly by. It could only ask the States for money, hat in hand, and not collect even enough to pay interest on the debt. It could only mutter futilely about foreign regulations against American shipping, and implore the States not to engage in tariff wars among themselves. It could neither coin money, regulate its value, nor prevent the States from cooking up monetary chaos. It was a government in name only, a monument to the doctrine of States' rights pushed to its logical extreme.

Creditors who wished to get their money back, merchants who sought to sell more goods at stable prices, free from foreign competition and domestic restrictions, shipowners and planters who longed for expanding foreign markets, and owners of western land had had their fill of the Articles of Confederation.

Nevertheless, they were a minority. They cannot have been more than a few thousand of the four million inhabitants of the United States then. Opposed to them, often on social as well as economic grounds, were the great mass of small farmers and frontiersmen on the land, the mechanics, the clerks and other workers in the towns. And to a small farmer perhaps 95 percent self-sufficient economically, or even to a mechanic in town with a good-sized garden and some livestock, the necessity for a stronger central government was not so obvious. The ways of King George III and his Parliament, who to them represented a strong government, were still in mind. "That government is best which governs least."

Hamilton and Madison knew, if some others did not, that a frontal attack on the Articles of Confederation would merely arouse State jealousies and the suspicions of the masses and end in defeat. A minority, however determined, must proceed cautiously.

Trial balloons to sound out sentiment for constitutional revision had not brought encouraging results. Virginia's invitation to the States to send delegates to a convention at Annapolis in 1786, presumably for proposing effective interstate regulations for commerce and navigation, brought representatives from only five of the thirteen States. The determined Hamilton refused to admit defeat, and talked the Annapolis meeting into a resolution which invited the States to choose delegates for a second convention to be held in Philadelphia the next year, 1787.

For the revisionists, that was progress, for they could read between the lines; for the public outside,

the Congress and the State legislatures, it seemed
harmless enough to send delegates empowered
merely to suggest "revisions" of the existing Articles
of Confederation in order to make them "adequate
to the exigencies of the Union," which revisions
would then be submitted both to Congress and to
the States for approval. There could not be much
harm in that, the more so since under the Articles
of Confederation an amendment must be approved
by every one of the thirteen States before becoming
part of the fundamental law.

To Hamilton's joy the States (except Rhode Island) responded with alacrity. Even the fact that
most of them empowered their delegates only to
revise the Articles, cannot have disturbed Hamilton
so much. He and his colleagues would cross that
bridge when they came to it.

The strategists of the pending Convention must
have watched the selection of delegates by the
States with some nervousness. Alarm at Virginia's
choice of Patrick Henry doubtless gave way to relief at Henry's refusal to attend, though the relief
was tempered by his undignified statement that he
"smellt a rat." The New England firebrand, Samuel
Adams, was not chosen; Tom Paine was battling
tyranny in Europe; Thomas Jefferson was likewise
abroad, as our representative to France; Willie
Jones, North Carolina delegate hot for democracy,
declined to serve. In short, with few exceptions, the

men whose democratic ardor was still at Revolutionary pitch either were not chosen as delegates, or refused to serve.

Twelve States, Rhode Island making no appointment, selected 62 delegates. Virginia and North Carolina had to name alternates for the three who declined to serve. Of the 62, seven never attended the Convention. Of the 55 who did attend, 29 were present for the opening session on May 25, 16 got there within the next 10 days, and the last straggler came along as late as August 6. Even so, many of the delegates were present only part of the time, whether through pressure of private business, despair of the Convention's success, or indifference.

* * *

For most of us, time and Fourth-of-July orations have blurred the proceedings of the Constitutional Convention and the qualities of the Founding Fathers. We have forgotten how human they were, and though human, how admirable. We too often think of the Convention as a meeting of disembodied spirits. We have placed the Fathers on pedestals, but have neglected to build foundations under them. A few more years, a few more thousand breast-beating, flag-waving orations, and the Founding Fathers will become chilly abstractions, lifeless and dull.

To have a bold and daring group of young men
meet such a fate does not appeal to me. There is still
too much to learn from them.

To be sure they were men of spirit, but they were
not disembodied spirits; they had roots in the soil
of eighteenth-century America; they owned to likes
and dislikes, to appetites and to humors; they viewed
some matters conservatively and others radically,
were frequently moved by prejudice, and harbored
ideas derived both from the prevailing public opinion and from their material interests.

There is no inconsistency in viewing them as did
Major William Pierce, delegate from Georgia, both
as human beings and as members of the "wisest
Council in the World." It sharpens our understanding of the Convention and the Constitution to see
them as an alert fellow-delegate saw them.

Major Pierce, the private "columnist" of the Convention, thus records that Hamilton was "rather a
convincing Speaker than a blazing Orator," sometimes disagreeably vain, whereas Madison was "A
Gentleman of great modesty,—with a remarkable
sweet temper." What is more, this leader in the
Convention (Madison), though long in public life,
was still acknowledged great by all, for "He blends
together the profound politician, with the Scholar."

Washington, of course, was already plainly destined for immortality, and so was Doctor Franklin,
then 82, "But what claim he has to the politician,
posterity must determine."

Roger Sherman of Connecticut seemed to Pierce odd, awkward, and handicapped by "that strange New England cant," but nevertheless possessed of a sound heart and head. He was one of the few delegates who had risen from low estate, having started as shoemaker, finally becoming an honored judge.

Livingston of New Jersey, a leader of the small State group, showed more "wit, than a strength of thinking," but his companion, Patterson, was "one of those kind of Men whose powers break in upon you, and create wonder and astonishment." As much might be said of Pennsylvania's James Wilson, among others. Gouverneur Morris, stylist of the Constitution, seemed a bit too charming for Pierce —"fickle and inconstant."

George Read of Delaware and Luther Martin of Maryland apparently bored the Major acutely by long-winded speeches, badly delivered. He had kinder things to say of some of the more obscure delegates' "good plain understanding," even if he was amazed by the religious enthusiasm of Delaware's Richard Bassett, "lately turned Methodist," but with "modesty enough to hold his Tongue." And as for one of his Georgia colleagues, William Houstoun, "Nature seems to have done more for his corporeal than mental powers." The Major could be tart on occasion.

Major Pierce's sketches are helpful, but of course the historical researches of Max Farrand and Charles A. Beard, among others, go more directly to the sources of behavior and attitude, sources in large part economic.

It does not seem to me a sin that man should acknowledge an economic interest in government. The men who framed the Constitution did not conceal the fact that their economic interests required a government capable of restoring the public credit, fostering commerce and manufactures, and in general protecting property.

Beard, after examining the economic interests of the Founding Fathers in his *An Economic Interpretation of the Constitution*, reveals that more than half of the 55 in attendance at the Convention were lawyers, that most of the delegates came from towns, on or near the coast, where money and property control was concentrated, that none of the delegates was by occupation and income a representative of the small farming or laboring classes, and that the overwhelming majority of delegates—at least five-sixths—"were immediately, directly, and personally interested in the outcome of their labors at Philadelphia, and were to a greater or less extent economic beneficiaries from the adoption of the Constitution."

That is to say, 40 of the 55 delegates attending the Convention owned public securities, 14 had sizable investments in lands for speculation, 24 had money out at interest, 15 were owners of slaves, and 11 drew their income from mercantile, manufacturing or shipping businesses. Two exceptions, however, are noteworthy: neither Hamilton nor Madison possessed enough property to benefit much financially from a strong national government, a fact which suggests that human motives are often complex and human rewards found in many fields other than the economic.

Adoption of the Constitution and establishment of a powerful national government restored a sinking public credit. The total domestic public debt at the same time approximated 60 million dollars, but the holders of that paper in the spring of 1787 saw the market going down and down until some of the paper sold as low as 20 to 1, and many thought it worthless. A return of 20 million dollars, Beard estimates, was the most the investors could expect under the Articles of Confederation. Under the new government and Hamilton's skillful financial plan, the domestic debt was funded at $60,789,914.18. To those who had put up the money to finance the Revolution, this much return seemed only justice. Unfortunately, in some States more than one-half of the paper, including soldiers' certificates, had passed into the hands of speculators at low figures. Some of the speculators, of course, became embarrassingly ardent in their approval of the new Constitution.

The sum of 60 million dollars, or a gain of 40 million dollars, does not seem impressive to a generation accustomed to read of billions. At that time, however, public securities represented a large proportion of all intangible wealth, and in some States totaled more than all the money at interest and on hand. Public security values of 60 million dollars may be compared with a total land value of around 400 million dollars for the United States in 1787; and with total exports averaging about 20 million dollars a year.

To the 11 delegates to the Convention who directly represented economic interests in mercantile, manufacturing and shipping businesses, the Constitution became not only a great document but a useful one, for they regarded it as a sure protection against foreign competition. Indeed, some of their names were attached to memorials to the First Congress, praying for discriminatory tariff laws. Though there is no evidence that labor and the consumer objected to heavy imports of foreign goods, the petitioners put their appeal on a broad basis, pointing to languishing trade and manufactures, to "the number of ... poor increasing for want of employment," and with a superior wisdom observing that "their countrymen have been deluded by an appearance of plenty; by the profusion of foreign articles which has deluged the country; and thus have mistaken excessive importation for a flourishing trade."

Those who owned western lands, or stock in land companies, felt with peculiar force the weaknesses of the Articles of Confederation, and the need for a strong national government. The lack of proper military protection, the weak fiscal position of the

government, and its general instability prevented
lands bought for speculation from appreciating at
the hoped-for rate. As Hugh Williamson, delegate
from North Carolina, wrote to Madison on June 2,
1788, "For myself, I conceive that my opinions are
not biassed by private Interest, but having claims
to a considerable Quantity of Land in the Western
Country, I am fully persuaded that the Value of
those Lands must be increased by an efficient federal
Government."

Frankly, it does come with something of a shock
to learn of the Maryland delegate who not only
owned the land on which the District of Columbia
was established, but who as a member of Congress
in 1789–91 served as one of the commissioners to lay
out the District. And the behavior of the New
Hampshire delegate who wrote home, while the
Convention was in session, urging New Hampshire
towns to buy up public paper and hold for a rise,
is perhaps open to question.

Episodes such as these are a little startling, but
they should not be too startling to men familiar
with the fact that government and constitutions
are only in part abstract. There is point to what
Beard says of the Philadelphia delegates: "As a
group of doctrinaires, like the Frankfort assembly
of 1848, they would have failed miserably; but as
practical men they were able to build the new government upon the only foundations which could be
stable: fundamental economic interests."

The delegates who gathered in Philadelphia on May 25, 1787, were determined, but cautious. Their knowledge of the temper of the country, and their sense of strategy, persuaded them to go into executive session, adopt a pledge of secrecy, record only the bare recital of motions and votes, and advise the Congress, the States, and the people of what they were about only when their labors were ended. So fearful were they of publicity that they even instructed a discreet colleague to accompany Doctor Franklin to dinners at which the old gentleman was likely, in a moment of enthusiasm, to reveal more than he should. But fortunately for historians, the pledge of secrecy was liberal enough to permit Madison, Pierce and a few others to keep diaries of the Convention, and from sources such as these it is possible to reconstruct much of what took place, and why.

Having settled the problem of secrecy, the Convention next considered how much revision of the Articles of Confederation would be necessary. It early became apparent, from the implications of the Virginia proposals, and the arguments of Hamilton, Madison, Randolph of Virginia, and others, that the Articles could not profitably be revised. They would have to be scrapped and a wholly new Constitution devised.

But what of the delegates whose instructions limited them to revising the Articles? "If the confederacy is radically wrong," argued Paterson of

New Jersey with great dignity, "let us return to our States and obtain larger powers, not assume them ourselves."

Randolph replied that he was not "scrupulous on the point of power." Hamilton contended that to propose a plan inadequate to the exigencies of union would be to sacrifice the end to the means. And most of the delegates agreed that the necessities of union were superior to literal logic. The Articles were discarded.

Nor did these bold young men stop there. Instead of having Congress send the new document to the State legislatures for approval, they asked Congress to go over the heads of the legislatures and appealed directly to the qualified voters for ratification. And finally, ignoring the clause in the Articles requiring unanimous approval for every amendment, they proposed that the new Constitution should take effect when approved by nine of the thirteen States. The Fathers, I fear, were stretching the liberal interpretation of the Articles beyond the breaking point, and using unconstitutional means to gain their end. As those who delight in paradox have since pointed out, the Constitution they established was in its origin unconstitutional.*

---

* "What they [the Convention] actually did, stripped of all fiction and verbiage, was to assume constituent powers, ordain a Constitution of government and of liberty, and demand a *plebiscite* thereon over the heads of all existing legally organized powers. Had Julius or Napoleon committed these acts they would have been pronounced coups d'etat."— Professor John W. Burgess, in *Political Science and Comparative Constitutional Law*, Vol. I, p. 105, as quoted by Beard.

The delegates to the Philadelphia Convention scrapped the Articles of Confederation not from caprice, or from the desire of powerful men to demonstrate their power, but simply because they saw no other way to establish the kind of government they believed necessary. They foresaw that Rhode Island, and perhaps other States, would not willingly ratify the new Constitution, therefore they provided for ratification by only nine States. They provided for ratification by State conventions rather than legislatures, because they knew the legislators would not willingly relinquish any of their power. And with special State conventions, the friends of the new Constitution would have a chance to confine the public discussion to the matter in hand, and conduct the necessary educational campaign.

Nevertheless, the victory of practical considerations over the logic of the Articles of Confederation was not easily won. After the Constitution had been submitted to the States for ratification, Hamilton and Madison had some strenuous arguing to do in *The Federalist* to defend their position. Madison, in words very like those used by Lincoln* years later, said to the strict constructionists: "Let them declare whether it was of most importance to the happiness of the people of America that the Articles of Con-

---

* In defense of actions which some thought were unconstitutional, Lincoln in a letter to A. G. Hodges on April 4, 1864, said: "Was it possible to lose the nation and yet preserve the Constitution? By general law, life and limb must be protected; yet, often a limb must be amputated to save a life, but a life is never wisely given to save a limb."

federation should be disregarded and an adequate
government be provided and the Union preserved;
or that an adequate government should be omitted
and the Articles of Confederation preserved."

The opposition was shaken but not silenced. In
the public letters of "Cornelius" in Massachusetts,
in December of 1787, there were references to "that
fundamental and solemn compact," followed by a
series of rhetorical questions to this effect: "If a
nation may so easily discharge itself from obligations
to abide by its most solemn fundamental compacts,
may it not with still greater ease do the same in
matters of less importance? And if nations may set
the example, may not particular states, citizens, and
subjects follow? What then will become of public
and private faith? . . .Has moral obligation no place
in civil government?"

But to return to the Convention: On the end to
be sought in the new Constitution, nearly all of the
delegates were in agreement. The conclusion is inescapable that they sought a strong and an efficient
national government. Their economic interests,
their social environment, their training and experience, and the inadequacy of the Articles of Confederation could lead only to that objective. Earlier historians and politicians who have made much of the
contests in the Convention between large and small
States, have ignored many of the votes in the Convention, the private utterances of many of the delegates, and the fact that dominant economic interests
even in those days were not segregated by State

lines. The contest was not between large and small
States for States' rights as opposed to a national
government, but a contest between large and small
States for control of the new government which both
groups wished to be national and strong.* "The truth
is," said Hamilton, "it is a contest for power, not
for liberty." And after all, the country was intimately
familiar with States' rights under the Articles of
Confederation, for that was nothing if not a States'
rights document, and what reason is there to believe
the Founding Fathers wished more of the same?

Indeed, within five days after the assembly had
convened, the delegates solemnly resolved "that a
national government ought to be established con-
sisting of a supreme legislative, executive, and judiciary." The vote was six to one for the resolution,
with one State's vote divided. The word "national"
was later struck out as likely to afford the opposition
too obvious a point of attack, but there remain in
the records the comments of Hamilton, Madison,
Gouverneur Morris and the other leaders to suggest
that the word "national" had not been erased from
their minds.†

* * *

---

* I realize that this is not the conventional view. Those who wish
to examine the supporting evidence for it will find it in the book soon
to be published by Mr. Irving Brant.
† Thus Hamilton, in 1787: "If it [the national government] were limited
at all, the rivalship of the States would gradually subvert it."
Thus Madison: "The States are every day giving proof that separate

However much a group of men may agree on a given end, controversy begins when it comes time to devise the means to that end. The Constitutional Convention was no exception. Though united in their desire to build a strong national government which would make private property secure, not all the delegates were equally interested in the same kind of property. Here was a source of potential conflict between northern merchants and manufacturers, for example, and southern planters, between those who stood to gain by protective tariffs, and those who didn't. Nevertheless, these were minor conflicts in the Convention as compared with the unanimity on the fundamental economic objectives. Necessarily there would be compromises on methods, but it is doubtful if these compromises, and the controversies which preceded them, were really as important as the early historians made them seem.

The Convention did not hesitate long over what was perhaps the basic questions of method before it, the question of how the Federal Government should give effect to its broad powers, whether through State governments or directly upon individual citizens.

---

regulations are more likely to set them by the ears than to attain the common object."

Thus Washington, during the Convention: "My wish is that the Convention may adopt no temporizing expedient, but probe the defects of the Constitution to the bottom and provide a radical cure whether they are agreed to or not." And again: "I do not conceive we can exist long as a nation without having lodged somewhere a power which pervades the whole Union in as energetic a manner as the authority of the state government extends over the several States."

The answer, quickly arrived at, was explained by
Madison in a letter to Jefferson shortly after the
Convention: "It was generally agreed," he wrote,
"that the objects of the Union could not be secured
by any system founded on the principle of a confederation of sovereign States. A voluntary observance
of the Federal law by all the members could never
be hoped for. A compulsive one could evidently
never be reduced to practice, and if it could, involved equal calamities to the innocent and the
guilty, the necessity of a military force, both obnoxi-
ous and dangerous, and, in general, a scene resem-
bling much more a civil war than the administration
of a regular government. Hence was embraced the
alternative of a government which, instead of
operating on the States, should operate without
their intervention on the individuals composing
them; and hence the change in the principle and
proportion of representation."

Strong words for one who in a few years was to
become an ardent States' rights man!

Had the Constitution operated on the States by
compulsion, civil strife would undoubtedly have followed quickly. Instead, the existence of both State
and Federal sovereignties was assumed, but with
by far the major sphere of power granted to the
Federal sovereignty. No State enactment could be
valid if in conflict with the Federal Constitution or
Federal statutes; Federal laws were to be enforced
by the judiciary of the whole land, State and Federal.

The precise boundaries of Federal and State sovereignties were not given, in part because no two men could agree on the location of those boundaries, in part because the majority of the delegates wished a strong national government but did not wish to say so too openly.

There was likewise general agreement that the new government must have ample power to defend the nation on land and sea, pay the national debt, defend property against such as Daniel Shays, and really enforce "domestic Tranquillity." None of the delegates advocated repudiation of the national debt; only one questioned the clause sustaining the validity of all outstanding obligations and contracts.

Not much argument was necessary to endorse the proposition that Congress should have the power to levy taxes, to regulate commerce with foreign nations and among the States, and to exercise whatever powers were implied in effectuating its enumerated functions. Likewise it was rather quickly agreed that the power to coin and regulate the value of money belonged to Congress, and should be denied individual States.

And as for democracy, only a few delegates had a kind word to say for it. On the contrary, Madison discoursed on the perils of majority rule, explaining that the great goal was "to secure the public good and private rights against the danger of such a faction and at the same time preserve the spirit and form of popular government." Elbridge Gerry of

Massachusetts said most of the troubles of the
country came from "the excess of democracy,"
Randolph of Virginia echoed him, and Hamilton,
advocating a life term for Senators, explained that
in every community there are the few and the many,
the few being rich and well-born, the others com-
prising the masses "who seldom judge or determine
right."

The reply of the Founding Fathers to the Sam
Adamses, the Patrick Henrys, the contemporary
advocates of "Let the people rule" was that ingenious, if somewhat optimistic, theory of checks and
balances.

It was in devising checks and balances, and in
developing the form of the Constitution, that the
delegates had their worst troubles. Madison, the
"Father of the Constitution," was well aware that
theories of government do not emerge full-blown
from the blue. Different individuals entertain different theories of government for a number of
reasons, but the dominant reason two times out of
three is economic.

Madison showed in *The Federalist* how the theories
of government which men hold are chiefly—not
solely, of course—emotional reactions to their property interests. Poor men wish government to do one
thing, rich men another; farmers wish a strong
government for one purpose, and a weak government
for another; industry wishes no government interference in this field, but a high degree of interference

in that sector; and what industry, or farmers, or labor, or their representative politicians wish government to do or not to do at one stage in a nation's history, may be and often is directly contrary to what they wish government to do or not to do at another stage.

From this diversity in interests, and from the danger of factions combining to form a reckless majority, the idea of a government of balanced powers arose. Probably the writings of Locke and Montesquieu helped the Founding Fathers grasp the notion the more readily, and of course the people as a whole at that time were on guard against dictatorship, having had their fill of George III. The Fathers were able skillfully to transmute that fear into approval of a system of checks and balances, the checks being directed especially against Congress and the State legislatures.

This outcome was achieved by letting the people elect the members of the House of Representatives, but having Senators elected by the State legislatures, and the President chosen by electors—presumably gentlemen of eminence and sound judgment—who in turn would be elected by the people. Under such an arrangement, it was pointed out in *The Federalist*, No. 60, "there would be little probability of a common interest to cement these different branches in a predilection for any particular class of electors." Or as Beard puts it, in the candid language of the historian rather than in the more soothing periods of the politician, "The economic corollary of this system is as follows: Property interests may, through their superior weight in power and intelligence, secure advantageous legislation whenever necessary, and they may at the same time obtain immunity from control by parliamentary majorities."

When to this system was added in later years a judicial control* unique in the art of government, the ingenuity of our forbearers had indeed reached new heights. Here were the executive, legislative and judicial branches scientifically poised against each other, and kept within limits imposed by both centripetal and centrifugal forces.

Unfortunately the theory has not worked out quite that way in practice, partly because the Founding Fathers did not foresee our two-party system, partly because their safeguards around the presidency and the Senate were later removed and direct election substituted.† But the fundamental weakness in the system was indicated many years later with superb cogency by an American President who was also a profound student of government and our

* For a discussion of this subject, see Chapter XIV.

† The seventeenth amendment, approved in 1913, provides for popular election of Senators. The present method of electing a President, by which the electoral college device set up in Article II, Section 1, is reduced to a formality, came into vogue more than a century ago by mutual consent but without benefit of amendment. Thus there seem to be at least two ways to amend the Constitution.

Constitution. Woodrow Wilson, in his *Constitutional Government in the United States*, wrote as follows:

Government is not a dead thing, but a living thing. It falls, not under the theory of the universe, but under the theory of organic life. It is accountable to Darwin, not to Newton. It is modified by its environment, necessitated by its tasks, shaped to its functions by the sheer pressure of life. No living thing can have its organs offset against each other as a check, and live. On the contrary, its life is dependent upon their quick and amicable community of purpose. Government is not a body of blind forces; it is a body of men, with highly differentiated functions no doubt, in our modern day of specialization, but with a common task and purpose. . . . There can be no successful government without leadership or without the intimate, almost instinctive co-ordination of the organs of life and action. This is not theory, but fact, and displays its force as fact, whatever theories may be thrown across its track.

Even in the Philadelphia Convention the theory of checks and balances had hard sledding, for when the smoke of controversy had disappeared, there remained a document which still gave tremendous powers to the legislature, both in its own sphere and in its influence over the executive by the right to override vetos and to impeach, and in its influence over the judiciary by the power to establish new courts, increase the number of judges, define jurisdiction, and in other ways.

The final document was indeed "a bundle of compromises," so far as the surface structure of government was concerned, and a far cry from the two plans upon which the delegates first concentrated, the Virginia plan put forth by Randolph and the New Jersey plan offered by Paterson. The Virginia plan proposed two houses of congress with members apportioned among the States on the basis of holding of land or free population. This congress was to elect the executive and to have broad legislative powers, even including the power to veto State laws.*

In contrast to the Virginia plan, Paterson's plan called for a single house of congress in which States, rather than people, were to be represented, and all States were to have an equal vote. Paterson, from a small State, admitted a lingering affection for the Articles of Confederation.

Despite the many compromises in the Constitution—including the slavery compromise which foreshadowed the tragic conflict of 1861—the significant

---

* Ironically, this power to veto State laws, strongly advocated by Madison and other Virginians at the Convention, but defeated because it seemed unworkable, was soon assumed by the federal judiciary—and against Virginia! A Virginia law permitting sequestration of debts due to the British, notably those London merchants to whom Virginia planters owed about $2,000,000, was declared unconstitutional on the ground that State laws which conflicted with the treaties of the United States were null and void. Justices Paterson and Wilson, both delegates to the Constitutional Convention, were members of the Supreme Court which delivered this blow to the Father of the Convention and his fellow-Virginians.

fact remains that the Fathers had so much determination, and so great a capacity for practical adjustments, that a living Constitution was brought forth, and a loose confederation of jealous States made a united nation. Throughout the proceedings of the Convention, throughout the private letters of the framers of the Constitution, one finds recurring that passion for unity, for sufficient national power to solve national problems, and for promotion of the General Welfare—as they defined it—which we still see shining through the preamble.

It is not to be denied that the Constitution they brought forth had in large part an economic base. The Founding Fathers could no more divorce themselves from their own economic interests than could a convention of farmers and laboring men, meeting for a comparable purpose, not to mention conventions of manufacturers, or dentists, or school teachers, or lawyers. Nevertheless, the economic interests of the Fathers did not blind them to the needs of a nation struggling to be born; or, if you prefer, constitutional protection of the economic interests represented by the Founding Fathers did not, in 1787, work undue hardship on less powerful economic interests in a nation endowed with a wide continent rich in resources.

Doubtless the delegates at the Constitutional Convention would be amazed to find the product of their labors still the fundamental law of the land. That this is so is because they conferred broad powers within a framework of representative government, and because they did not deny to future generations the right to modify the document as they saw fit. A rigid, inorganic structure could never have weathered so many emergencies.

National power to solve national problems was intended by the Founding Fathers. They knew what the national problems were in 1787, and they knew what they were about in creating a power to solve them. What the national problems might be a generation hence, a century hence, no man could say. The power had been created, to be utilized by future generations as they required.

"A government ought to contain in itself," wrote Alexander Hamilton in Article 31 of *The Federalist*, "every power requisite to the full accomplishment of the objects committed to its care, and to the complete execution of the trusts for which it is responsible, free from every other control but a regard to the public good and to the sense of the people."

And to those of his countrymen who wanted a wooden not a living Constitution, Hamilton said further in Article 34 of *The Federalist*: "In pursuing our inquiry, we must bear in mind that we are not to confine our view to the present period, but to look forward to remote futurity. Constitutions of civil government are not to be framed upon a calculation of existing exigencies, but upon a combination of these with the probable exigencies of ages, according to the natural and tried course of human affairs. Nothing, therefore, can be more fallacious than to infer the extent of any power, proper to be lodged in the national government, from an estimate of its immediate necessities. There ought to be a CAPACITY to provide for future contingencies as they may happen; and as these are illimitable in their nature, it is impossible safely to limit that capacity."

Conceivably a provision created in 1787 to protect private property in the form of slaves might be utilized a century later to protect private property against income taxes. The question of how a power may be used can never be answered by one generation for another generation. Each generation must summon up what wisdom it can, and solve its own problems. The axiom that a power which is created for one social purpose may ultimately be used for a contrary purpose should heighten each new generation's sense of responsibility, but no device of man, known or discoverable, can long prevent a people from working out its salvation as an overwhelming majority deems best.

The men who wrote the Constitution did not pretend that they had achieved perfection, even for their generation. They were none too sanguine that the gears would mesh, and the machinery move. They could not be too specific in granting powers, for the simple reason that they could not foresee the future. And powers broadly expressed, of course, give rise to innumerable interpretations. Of the hundreds of illustrations, let me cite one:

In the closing days* of the Convention Franklin proposed that Congress should have power to build canals as well as post roads. There was objection from delegates who did not see how their States would benefit. Madison stepped into the breach by suggesting a less specific and far broader grant of power, namely, that Congress have power "to grant charters of incorporations." Randolph seconded him, and Wilson of Pennsylvania came strongly to his support, observing that "It is necessary to prevent a State from obstructing the general welfare."

When it was objected that such a power might permit the formation of mercantile monopolies, Wilson replied that the power to create mercantile monopolies was included in the power of Congress to regulate trade. Colonel Mason of Virginia didn't think so, and there the matter rested.† Madison's general motion did not come to vote, but the earlier motion, limited to canals, was defeated, eight States to three.

Thus the question remains: How much power did the framers intend Congress to have over trade? And the corresponding question: How broad is a broad power? The delegates at Philadelphia did not put the answers in the Constitution.

A unanimous convention is always more pleasing to the eye than a divided convention. The leading strategists at Philadelphia in 1787 knew that, and

* On September 14, 1787, three days before adjournment.
† Two days later Mason admitted Wilson was probably right and gave his fear of that power as a reason for refusing to sign the Constitution.

knew also the importance of presenting a united
front to the country. Doctor Franklin was chosen
by the leaders to make the appeal for unanimity on
the closing day. In honeyed words the old philosopher delivered his appeal to reason and to patriotism: "I can not help expressing a wish that every
member of the Convention who may still have objec-
tions to it, would with me, on this occasion doubt
a little of his own infallibility, and to make manifest
our unanimity, put his name to this instrument."

But with such outstanding delegates as Gerry of
Massachusetts and Randolph of Virginia among
the dissenters, even Franklin's persuasiveness was
wasted. The leaders, however, were equal to the
occasion. Franklin then moved that the signing be
done in this form: "Done in Convention by the
unanimous consent of *the States* present," etc. The
form, if not the substance, of unanimity was thus
achieved, and the document was so submitted to
the Congress and the States. Of the 55 delegates
present at one or more sessions, however, only 39
signed, and 16 refused to.

Then followed months of intensive campaigning for
the Constitution in the States, as ratifying conventions were chosen. Press, pamphlets and personal
correspondence poured out for and against the new
plan. Madison, Hamilton and Jay contributed
heavily through *The Federalist*. Weak supporters had
to be buttressed, vociferous opponents answered.
The wounds of State pride had to be assuaged, and

the fears of a liberty-loving people allayed by assurance that amendments would speedily be submitted guaranteeing the Rights of Man which had been stated so boldly in the Declaration of Independence. For one reason or another the Philadelphia assembly had neglected to include any Bill of Rights in the body of the Constitution, and had even voted down a motion to guarantee freedom of the press, when presented by Pinckney and Gerry. As Roger Sherman said, the guarantee was unnecessary.

From the turmoil of the State ratifying conventions, however, there emerged firm declarations that they would approve the Constitution only on the understanding that a Bill of Rights would be added as promptly as possible. From New Hampshire, Virginia, New York, North Carolina and Rhode Island came the strongest of these provisos. Had Thomas Jefferson been a member of the Philadelphia Convention, perhaps the Bill of Rights would have been at the very core of the original Constitution, rather than an afterthought insisted upon by a minority of State ratifying conventions.

As the record reveals, the First Congress combined the requests of the State conventions in 12 amendments and submitted them to the States on March 4, 1789, and 10 of them became the law of the land in 1791. The first two of the 12 submitted, dealing with the number of representatives and denying Congress the right to raise its own salary until an election had intervened, were not approved. No vote on any of the 12 was returned to the Congress by Massachusetts, Connecticut, or Georgia.

When ratification of the original Constitution was being celebrated in Philadelphia in 1788, James Wilson, Founding Father and later Justice of the Supreme Court, expressed his enthusiasm with perhaps understandable exaggeration: "A whole people exercising its first and greatest power—performing an act of sovereignty, original and unlimited!" His words have since become part of the standard repertory of thousands of orators, and are embalmed in the legal fiction which requires that the Constitution be viewed as the will of the whole people.

I do not see that it will injure any American, however, to know that there is often a distinction between rhetoric, political or legal, and statements of fact. Apparently not more than 5 percent of "the whole people" in 1787–88 actually voted either for or against the Constitution. Reliable historians estimate that 160,000 persons voted on the election of delegates to the State ratifying conventions, and that probably not more than 100,000 of these were in favor of the Constitution, or about one in every six adult white males in the United States in 1788. The other five of those six would be heard from later, through their economic "descendants," in the time of Jefferson and Jackson. But meanwhile a Constitution had been adopted, a more perfect Union formed, a representative form of government guaranteed and a mighty Nation launched.

* * *

Soon after the Constitutional Convention had adjourned, a friend complimented Gouverneur Morris on the new document. "You have made a good Constitution," he said.

"That," replied Morris, "depends on how it is construed."

Chapter XIV

THE ELDER STATESMEN

THE framers of the Constitution left a good many questions unanswered. One of the greatest of these, still troubling us, is the power of the Supreme Court to pass on acts of Congress.

It is not easy to divorce this question from controversy. It arose in controversy, and has reappeared throughout our history as great issues have divided men into two camps. Attempts by the Court to decide controversial issues have usually added fresh fuel to the controversy. It is then that proposals to curb the power of the Court come forth. Those who agree with the Court's decision usually denounce advocates of curbing the Court as unpatriotic, a menace to our liberties, etc. Unfortunately for consistency, within a few years the friends of the Court sometimes become its bitterest critics, and the former critics its staunchest supporters.

Men steeped in the law, observing these tides of controversy which usually recede leaving the Court untouched, come to the happy conclusion that this proves the infallibility of the Court and the law. It does nothing of the sort, of course, for reasons which will be apparent later, but it does prove the strength of our emotional attachment to the Supreme

Court as an institution. That is a fact of which most Americans are aware, and of which the members of the Court itself cannot be ignorant. This emotional attachment is the source of the Court's tremendous power, a power perhaps greater than the power of money or troops in a democracy, but a power which lays upon the Court heavy responsibilities.

Some of our emotional attachment to the Court comes from our admiration for members of the Court, for their integrity and freedom from narrow partisan bias; some comes from the human longing for stability and certainty, which the decisions of the Court so often seem* to provide; but originally, I think, our emotional attachment to the Court came from the tendency to identify it, rather than the President or the Congress, with the Constitution.

The Court itself set in motion this tendency to regard judges, rather than executives or legislators, as the protectors of the Constitution. Surprising as it may seem, nothing in the Constitution specifically says that the courts, rather than executives or legislators, shall have the final say on what is or is not constitutional. I think all who are familiar with the constitutional history of the United States agree that the Constitution does not, in so many words, give the Supreme Court the power to pass upon the constitutionality of acts of Congress. Whether the Constitution gives the Court this power by implica-

---

* "Certainty generally is illusion, and repose is not the destiny of man." —Mr. Justice Holmes.

tion, is another question. Most lawyers and historians
believe that the power is implied in Article III,
Section 2, of the Constitution,* and that Marshall,
in the famous Marbury case, did no more than state
the irrefutable logic of the implication.

The question never really came up in the Constitutional Convention. There is no record of any
resolution giving the judiciary power to annul acts of
Congress. The nearest to it was a proposal to make
the President and the Supreme Court a council of
revision with joint veto powers over acts of Congress,
but this proposal was soon rejected, and in any case
was not the same as judicial review. What the
Founding Fathers intended, therefore, we can never
know. If they intended to have the Supreme Court
pass upon the constitutionality of acts of Congress,
they failed to express their intent specifically in the
Constitution.†

What the framers of the Constitution failed to say
in 1787, John Marshall said in 1803 as Chief Justice.

* "The judicial power shall extend to all cases, in law and equity, arising
under this Constitution. . . ."

† Albert J. Beveridge, in his *Life of Marshall*, after examining the records
of the Convention finds that the delegates touched on this subject of
judicial review but notably failed to agree. Franklin, Madison (with
reservations), Bedford, Mercer, Dickinson, and Charles Pinckney said
the courts should not have the power to pass upon acts of Congress.
Gerry, Rufus King, George Mason, Gouverneur Morris, James Wilson
and Luther Martin thought the courts either should have this power or
would assume it. Of these latter delegates, Gerry, Mason and Martin
refused to sign the Constitution. Alexander Hamilton, however, argued
in *The Federalist* for something very close to judicial supremacy, and
recent researches of Charles Warren show that the subject was discussed
in several of the State ratifying conventions, though inconclusively.

In the famous Marbury case, in which an Adams appointee tried in vain to obtain his commission as justice of the peace from the new Jefferson administration, Chief Justice Marshall* held that while Marbury had a right to his commission, the Court had no constitutional power to compel the executive branch to deliver it, the act of Congress to the contrary notwithstanding.

From that springboard Marshall leaped to the conclusion that the Court had the power to pass on any act of Congress which might be challenged in the courts. In convincing words he argued that in a government of limited powers, under a written Constitution, "It is emphatically the province and duty of the judicial department to say what the law is," and that "a law repugnant to the Constitution is void." In short, Marshall concluded, somebody has to decide whether or not acts of Congress are constitutional, and the judiciary ought not to shrink from its duty.

To the Federalists Marshall's argument seemed unanswerable; to Jefferson and his followers, Marshall was just another Federalist, one of those who Jefferson said had "retired into the judiciary as a stronghold."

Jefferson agreed there must be an ultimate arbiter somewhere, but why should it be the Court or even

---

* Marshall, a vigorous Federalist, served as Secretary of State under Adams, and on January 20, 1801, was appointed Chief Justice to succeed Oliver Ellsworth, resigned. From January 20 to March 4, 1801, Marshall held both offices.

the Congress? Why not the people? Whose Constitution was it, if not the people's? Madison said much the same thing, though he at one time thought the "meaning of the Constitution may as well be ascertained by the legislative as by the judicial authority."

Marshall himself changed his mind on this subject. At the Virginia convention to ratify the new Constitution in 1788, according to his biographer, Beveridge, Marshall said "if Congress should pass an unconstitutional law the courts would declare it void." A few years later, as an attorney arguing a case before the Supreme Court, Marshall said "the judicial authority can have no right to question the validity of a law unless such a jurisdiction is expressly given by the Constitution." In 1803, Marshall the Chief Justice in the Marbury case, reversed Marshall the attorney. And in 1804, apparently both angered and frightened by the impeachment proceedings against his colleague, Justice Chase, Marshall declared, in a letter to Chase: ". . . I think the modern doctrine of impeachment should yield to an appellate jurisdiction in the legislature. A reversal of those legal opinions deemed unsound by the legislature would certainly better comport with the mildness of our character than a removal of the Judge who has rendered them unknowing of his fault." That is, let Congress review, perhaps repass, statutes invalidated by the Supreme Court.

I do not cite the above to detract from Marshall's

greatness. Marshall's inconsistencies, which can be matched by the inconsistencies of all men, high or low, in every age, cannot diminish the value of his services to the United States in its formative period. Perhaps more than any other man then living, Marshall worked to make the United States a nation. He believed we could only achieve that "more perfect Union" through the use of broad national powers. He steered the Court's course accordingly. Without Marshall, or some one like him, we might not long have remained one nation.

It may be that to some extent Marshall, in the Marbury case, was fighting Jefferson and his party, partly for personal reasons, partly because of a passionate belief that Federalist principles were more in the general welfare than Jeffersonian principles. It may also be that Marshall, as Chief Justice of the Court in days when it had very little prestige, was anxious to persuade the people that the judiciary deserved both prestige and power. Finally, it may be that Marshall sought to stave off a growing sense of power in Congress and to establish, in the judiciary, an effective check upon radical legislation.

Whatever his motives, Marshall established a principle which ever since has been used by the Supreme Court and approved by most* of the people much of the time.

Marshall himself never employed the power to overrule an act of Congress after the Marbury case,

* Except, of course, Jefferson, Jackson, Lincoln, Theodore Roosevelt and their followers.

though constitutional questions were ruled on in 62 of the 1215 cases decided by the Supreme Court during the years Marshall was Chief Justice, 1801–35. Not until 1857, in the Dred Scott case, did the Court declare invalid an act of Congress, the Missouri Compromise Act of 1820.

Immediately after the Civil War the Court began to assert its power over acts of Congress more and more frequently. In the first 50 years of its existence, the Court handed down a decision invalidating an act of Congress in only one case; in the next 50 years, there were 19 such cases; and in the last 46 years, there have been 49 such cases. In the 15 years between 1920 and 1935 the Court nullified more acts of Congress than in the first 100 years of its existence. These 69 decisions handed down during the first 146 years of the Court's existence have invalidated 73 different provisions of law,* ranging from one phrase to an entire statute. In addition, the Supreme Court has declared unconstitutional more than 400 State laws.

Despite Marshall's logic, the Court has always said it was reluctant to pass on the constitutionality of an act of Congress. But the Court has also, as in the Dred Scott case and others, passed on the constitutionality of an act of Congress when it did not need to.

Its freedom of choice here is considerable, and it permits the Court to exercise the prerogatives of

* As of February 10, 1936.

statesman as well as judge. Freedom of choice in any field invites difference of opinion, as the number of dissenting opinions on constitutional questions testifies.

Thus the Supreme Court handed down unanimous decisions in 25 of the 69 cases referred to above as invalidating provisions of national law, but divided in 44 of these cases. Of the 25 cases, except for the Marbury case and the Schechter decision of 1935, and perhaps one or two others, few today seem historic. The 44 cases in which the Court divided, on the other hand, include the most controversial and the most historic cases ever decided by the Court. The Dred Scott case, the legal tender cases, the Slaughterhouse case, the income tax case, the child labor cases, the minimum wage case, the gold clause decision, Hoosac Mills—all these and others of the 44 were cases which involved great issues on which the people themselves had differed, and to which the judges, in the rôle of statesmen, necessarily brought similar differences of opinion.*

* * *

The basic problem before the Supreme Court on constitutional questions has usually been to deter-

---

* I realize that this view differs from that sometimes expressed by the Court. In the Hoosac Mills case Justice Roberts, speaking for the majority, declared that the Court doesn't really assume a power to overrule

mine how broad, vague phrases should apply to specific, concrete situations. It would be hard to find broader phrases than those used by the framers of the Constitution in conferring upon Congress the right to regulate commerce, for instance, and to tax and spend to provide for the general welfare.*

Within the broad language of such powers the Supreme Court has necessarily exercised much freedom of choice. I say "necessarily" because I do not see how it could do otherwise, given the task of applying a broad grant of power to a specific situation. Thus Marshall construed national powers broadly; Taney in the main construed them narrowly; and so the pendulum has swung back and forth, ever since.

The broad constructionists not only interpreted the expressed powers in the Constitution broadly, but agreed that many incidental powers were im-

---

or control Congress; all it does, when the constitutionality of an act of Congress is questioned, is its plain duty—"to lay the Article of the Constitution which is invoked beside the statute which is challenged, and to decide whether the latter squares with the former." The only power of the Court, "if such it may be called," Justice Roberts continues, "is the power of judgment." I fear Justice Roberts is too modest, however. To the layman the situation seems more accurately described by Justice Stone, speaking for the minority in the same case, when he writes: "The only check upon our own exercise of power is our own sense of self-restraint."

* In Article I, Section 8: "The Congress shall have power:

"To lay and collect taxes, duties, imposts and excises, to pay the debts and provide for the common defence and general welfare of the United States; . . . . "To regulate commerce with foreign nations, and among the several States, and with the Indian tribes."

plied in the expressed powers; that is, since Congress has the power to regulate commerce, it, by implication, has the power to set up whatever agencies may be necessary to execute the expressed power to regulate commerce. The narrow constructionists, on the other hand, have not only tended to interpret the expressed powers narrowly, but have also in effect denied many implied powers and substituted what Mr. Irving Brant calls "implied limitations."

Marshall believed a strong national government was intended by the Founding Fathers. While not denying the existence of the States as entities, he made it plain in many decisions that the National Government was the superior sovereignty. A broad grant of power, he thought, ought to remain a broad grant of power, despite the possibility of abuses of such power. "Questions of power," he wrote, "do not depend upon the degree to which it is exercised. If it exists at all, it may be exercised to the utmost extent."

Since Marshall's time, however, the power of the Federal Government, as well as of the State governments, has been challenged and often curtailed by great private economic powers acting through the courts. To illustrate this, and to illustrate how judicial interpretations change from time to time, we may examine the high spots in the checkered history of the commerce clause.

When Marshall was Chief Justice a case involving a steamboat monopoly between New York City and

Elizabethtown, N. J., came before the Court. The commerce clause was invoked. Was a steamboat company engaged in commerce? If so, could Congress lay down rules for its operation?

First, as to the word "commerce." Was that broad enough to include navigation? Marshall thundered a judicial "Yes!" without hesitation. Commerce was not merely traffic, or buying and selling; it was also navigation, and it might later be many other things as well. The Constitution had not said otherwise, had it? As for the word "regulate," Marshall assumed it to mean the power to govern if it meant anything at all.

What Marshall's liberal interpretations of the commerce clause did was to give the green light to a developing national commerce and keep it free from interruption by the States. Necessarily, the word "commerce" came to include activities the Founding Fathers did not even dream of. And the Court, particularly under the broad constructionists, blessed the new activities.

But the word "regulate," in the decisions of the narrow constructionists, met a different fate. Marshall's successors, generations later, after duly laying the commerce clause beside acts of Congress which had been challenged by large corporate interests, decided that the clause did not so much confer a power to govern as a power to foster, protect, and promote commerce.

Nor did the narrow constructionists stop there.

Having altered the power to govern to a power merely
to foster and protect, they then, in the Sugar Trust
case of 1895, eliminated from the word "commerce"
even those activities Marshall had said it plainly
included, such as buying and selling. Instead, said
the Court in 1895, the commerce clause gives Congress power only over interstate transportation.*

For years many people interested in improving
industrial conditions, and particularly in remov-
ing the blight of child labor, had been following
these decisions of the Supreme Court on the commerce clause. At least, they thought, the Court says
Congress has power over interstate transportation.
The products of child labor certainly move in interstate transportation. Why not correct the evil by
utilizing the Congressional power to regulate interstate transportation?

Congress agreed, in 1916, but the Court offered a
vigorous, if divided, objection in 1918. The Act of
1916 forbade the shipment in interstate commerce
of child-labor products. But, said the Court after
duly laying the statute questioned beside the com-

* The Court also said in this decision, though not unanimously, that
while the Sugar Trust was plainly in violation of the Sherman Anti-
Trust Act, Congress could not break up such a monopoly because to do
so would be to invade the police powers of the States. Manufacturing
sugar, it said, is a purely local activity. The majority refused to be im-
pressed by the fact that local manufacture could rarely create a monopoly without nation-wide distribution and sale of the product. For a pene-
trating discussion of the trend I am indicating above, see Professor
Corwin's book, *The Twilight of the Supreme Court*.

merce clause of the Constitution, the commerce
clause fails to include the power sought. Commerce
is not what John Marshall said it was; commerce is
merely transportation, and transportation is *separate*
from the act of manufacture, a purely local activity.*

While still reeling from that blow, the foes of child
labor next discovered the Court in the same opinion
placing the Child Labor Act beside the tenth amendment to the Constitution. This time the Court
found that the act was an invasion of powers reserved to the States.

To make such a discovery, however, Justice Day
in the majority opinion had to amend the tenth
amendment somewhat. He inserted the word "expressly," making the amendment read, "The powers
not (expressly) delegated to the United States by the
Constitution ... are reserved to the States, respec-
tively, or to the people."

* This astounding decision of the Court of course does not stop at *inter-
preting* the law: it writes new law without benefit of Congress or constitutional convention. What it says, in vivid contrast to what the
Founding Fathers said and did, is that the power of Congress to regulate
commerce may be emasculated by the Court whenever the Court thinks
State powers are likely to be diminished. Yet in case after case before
and since the Child Labor case the Court has said that of course the
Federal power is supreme, else we have no nation. As recently as February 3, 1936, Justice Stone, speaking for a unanimous Court in United
States v. State of California, involving application of the Safety Appli-
ance Act to a belt-line railroad owned and operated by California,
summed up in these words: "The sovereign power of the States is necessarily diminished to the extent of the grants of power to the Federal
Government in the Constitution." In other words, the tail goes with
the hide.

Justice Day's amendment to the tenth amendment made it possible for him to argue that since the Constitution does not *expressly* give Congress the power to prohibit the transportation of the products of child labor from State to State, the Child Labor Act obviously invades the reserved rights of the States over internal affairs.

Justice Holmes, speaking for the minority in a famous dissent, expressed his amazement at the majority view. "I should have thought," he wrote, "that the most conspicuous decisions of this Court had made it clear that the power to regulate commerce and other constitutional powers could not be cut down or qualified by the fact that it might interfere with the carrying out of the domestic policy of any state." Admitting the right of the States to control their purely internal affairs, "when they seek to send their products across the State line they are no longer within their rights."

Would the majority deny to Congress and the States together even that power over commerce which originally belonged to the individual States under the Articles of Confederation? Is the majority view plainly what the Founding Fathers intended, and what the Constitution said?

The Constitution, said the five majority Justices in effect, is what *we* say it is.

Thus it is unconstitutional to regulate or prohibit the shipment in interstate commerce of the products of child labor, but it is perfectly constitutional to regulate or prohibit the shipment in interstate commerce of narcotics, diseased cattle, women for immoral purposes, stolen automobiles, adulterated food, lottery tickets and prize-fight pictures.

What this child labor decision and preceding decisions of the Court did, as has been pointed out by Doctor Corwin, was to create a government vacuum, a legal no-man's-land in which favored economic interests could do as they pleased without intervention of either State or Federal government. First the Court gave Congress power to regulate national commerce, and prevent intervention by the States; but then the Court said (in this Child Labor case) that Congress could not exercise this power because to do so would invade the reserved rights of the States.

"So the States," Doctor Corwin comments, "which, without challenge, originally possessed this power, have now lost it by virtue of having delegated it to Congress, but Congress has never received it!"

When a constitutional grant of power becomes a judicial denial of power, we have the beginning of the end of government. We may have, it is true, greater freedom for certain important vested interests, but at the cost of the masses of the people and certainly at the cost of the fundamental purposes of the Founding Fathers.

Thus the process of laying an act of Congress alongside the appropriate section of the Constitution produces interesting but contradictory results. One generation's meat is another generation's poison. The Constitution fades into the background, and judicial interpretation comes up front. That strong national government for which the Fathers labored is by judicial interpretation first made strong, then weak, as one word of a constitutional grant of power is liberally construed, another narrowly construed. In consequence powerful economic interests grab the privileges of government and evade the responsibilities, while great masses of the people are consigned to a legal no-man's-land.

The language, "even of a Constitution," seems to mean different things in different periods, and even different things to different men in the same period.

* * *

The oscillations of the Supreme Court between the two poles of broad construction and narrow construction reflect in some degree the economic and social philosophies of the individuals in the Court, and in some degree the trend of the times. When the Court is successful in reflecting the trends and the needs of the times, as Marshall was, the problems of government are not so difficult; but when the Court either mistakes or lags behind in understanding the economic and social trends of the times, then the problems of government—and of the people living with that government—become almost insuperable.

Taney, in the Dred Scott case, made a tragic error in statesmanship. He need not have made it at all. His primary error was in assuming that a judicial decision could solve a fundamental economic and social problem. His secondary error was in his choice of a solution—States' rights. I think the same error in statesmanship has been made by the Court in other important cases on which the Court itself divided.

Concepts created for one purpose, linger on to plague the nation after the initial purpose has long since vanished. States' rights, born of a popular passion for individual liberty in the time of Jefferson, in the time of Taney became a shield for the right to own slaves, and since the Civil War a shield behind which a nation-wide corporation may pose as a purely local activity. The potency of States' rights as a political red herring has long since passed, but its potency as a legal red herring is still great.

But concepts created for one purpose may also be perverted to different and far less worthy purposes. Thus, due process of law, which to the Founding Fathers meant simply a fair trial, in the last 50 years has been accepted by the Court as an effective barrier to progressive legislation either by State governments or by the Federal Government.

So to broad versus narrow construction the Court has added the process of judicial invention. The modern interpretation of "due process of law" is a

brilliant example. The modern interpretation of the
tenth amendment is perhaps another. The modern
interpretation of the general welfare clause seems to
combine the best features of both judicial construction and judicial invention.

The result is a judicial freedom of choice un-
paralleled in our history. From the 40,000 decisions
the Supreme Court has handed down since 1789,
it may select a variety of precedents in order to
sanction, within rather broad limits, its latest interpretation of the Constitution. What the Constitution
has failed to say, at least one of the 40,000 decisions
has probably said.

The gravity of the problem before the Court can
hardly be overestimated. It can, by relying upon one
line of precedents rather than another, shut its eyes
to fundamental economic and social trends. It can
do this, but it will be at the cost of the faith of the
people of the United States, and ultimately at the
cost, I fear, of the Court itself.

It has lately had this problem before it in con-
struing the general welfare clause of the Constitution.
Mr. Irving Brant, in an unpublished manuscript
he has been kind enough to show me, observes that
Justice Roberts in the Hoosac Mills decision has cut
the effective use of the welfare clause down almost to
zero* by denying Congress the implied power to

* "Powerful and ingenious minds, taking, as postulates, that the powers
expressly granted to the government of the Union are to be contracted,
by construction, into the narrowest possible compass, and that the origi-

attach conditions to the use of Federal money, and by substituting, instead, implied limitations on the power of Congress. Like Justice Day in the Child Labor case, Justice Roberts in the Hoosac Mills case in effect wrote the word "expressly" into the tenth amendment.

The power of amending the Constitution, it seems to me, ought to be left to the people. It is true that a few members of the First Congress tried to write such a change into the tenth amendment before submitting it to the States for ratification, but their effort was decisively defeated by the Congress. Furthermore, the father of the general welfare clause, Roger Sherman of Connecticut, made it plain by word and deed that the power to promote the general welfare necessarily was a broad power, which included many corollary powers subject to change as the composition of the general welfare itself changed.

The contrast between the views of the author of the general welfare clause and the views of the majority of the Court in the Hoosac Mills case is presented by Mr. Brant as follows: "The Court in emasculating the General Welfare clause held that the money power involved no other powers. The

---

nal powers of the States are retained, if any possible construction will retain them, may, by a course of well digested, but refined and metaphysical reasoning, founded on these premises, explain away the Constitution of our country, and leave it a magnificent structure indeed to look at, but totally unfit for use."—Chief Justice Marshall, in concluding his opinion for the Court in Gibbons v. Ogden, in 1824.

author of the General Welfare clause said it involved many other powers. The Court said the power to spend money was subordinate to other powers. The author of the General Welfare clause said it was the most important of all the powers, and was granted, even under the Confederation, 'in the expectation that it would in all cases have its effect.' The Supreme Court said Congress could not use money to achieve a purpose within the reserved powers of the States. The author of the General Welfare clause advocated the use of federal funds to establish a national university, a subject more completely within the reserved rights of the States than agriculture, which is bound up with interstate commerce. To summarize the situation, it appears that the one interpretation of the General Welfare clause for which there is no historical warrant whatever, and no warrant in logic, is the interpretation made by six justices of the United States Supreme Court in 1936."

The General Welfare clause is dead! Long live the General Welfare clause!

* * *

It is difficult to know whether we have, in the commerce and welfare clauses, to name only two of the broad constitutional grants of power, a barrier or a highway.* It is likewise difficult to know what government can or cannot do, so long as the judiciary has so extraordinary a freedom of choice in approving or condemning legislative acts, whether its freedom derives from construction, precedents or judicial invention.

And yet, I believe that the Court will in due time convert some of the worst legal barriers into the broad highways the Founding Fathers thought they were building in 1787. I hold to this belief for two reasons: First, because the Court has frequently changed its mind in the past; second, because there will be no acceptable alternative before it.

In at least 60 cases the Supreme Court has definitely overruled its own previous decision or decisions. In four additional cases the minority pointed out that the majority opinion had the effect of overruling previous decisions. In 14 cases the Court, while not definitely overruling a previous decision, so qualified the principle of the prior case that it in fact was overruled. And in cases too numerous to mention the Court has handed down decisions which can be reconciled with earlier decisions only by the exercise of a kind of involved legal reasoning which

---

* Justice White, in addressing the American Bar Association in 1914, spoke as follows: "There is great danger, it seems to me, to arise from the constant habit which prevails where anything is opposed or objected to, of resorting without rhyme or reason to the Constitution as a means of preventing its accomplishment, thus creating the general impression that the Constitution is but a barrier to progress instead of being the broad highway through which alone true progress may be enjoyed."

to the modern scientific mind seems an echo from the Middle Ages.

A few examples will serve to illustrate how the Court refuses to adhere slavishly to that ancient legal doctrine of *stare decisis*, or, freely translated, "to stand on decided cases."

Back in 1825 the Court said the admiralty jurisdiction of the Federal Government extends only to water within the ebb and flow of the tide, but in 1852 jurisdiction was extended to all public navigable lakes and rivers where commerce is carried on between the States.

An indicted person, said the Court in 1896, must be arraigned and given an opportunity to plead to the indictment, and this fact must appear on the record. Said the Court in 1914: No formal arraignment or plea is necessary.

To seize a man's private papers for use as evidence against himself, the Court declared in 1886, compels him to be a witness against himself and is therefore a violation of the fourth and fifth amendments. 1904: It depends on how competent the evidence is. 1914: Illegally seized papers cannot be used where the owner has made a reasonable application for their return. 1928: Evidence illegally secured by wiretapping is admissible.

Corporations created by one State using the courts of another were, in 1898, held not to be "within the jurisdiction" of the latter State within the meaning of the clause, "No State shall ... deny to any per-

son *within its jurisdiction* the equal protection of the
laws" clause appears in the Fourteenth Amendment.* In, however, the Court held a foreign corporation be "within the jurisdiction" of the State in
which it suing, and so entitled to equal protection of
the law of that State.

Massachusetts, said the Supreme Court in 1928,
could not tax royalties received from patents.
Georgia, said the Court in 1932, could tax royalties
on copyrights.

Prices, the Court had decreed in many cases
through the years, may not be regulated by statute,
but in 1876 the Court decided that in the case of
businesses affected with a public interest, such as
grain elevators and warehouses, prices may be so
regulated. Fire insurance businesses, the Court
added in 1914, also come within this category. Theaters and similar places of entertainment, however,
the Court said in 1927, are not clothed with a public
interest so far as the price of admission is concerned.
Nevertheless and notwithstanding, said the Court
in 1935 in the Nebbia case, prices may be regulated
under the police powers of a State whether or not the
business is affected with a public interest.

Utah may restrict the hours of labor in mines and
smelters, the Court said in 1898, but New York
(said the Court in 1905) cannot restrict the hours of

---

* When this amendment was approved, in 1868, everybody thought
it was designed to protect the rights of Negroes and emasculate
the political and economic power of the leaders in the late Confederacy.

labor in a bakery. Oregon, the Court held in 1908, could restrict the hours of labor of women in a laundry, and even (in 1917) the hours of work of all employees in mills, factories or manufacturing establishments. But the District of Columbia, said the Court in 1923, may not fix minimum wage standards for women, whereas New York, the Court decided in 1924, might legally limit the hours of labor of women in restaurants.*

Where a legislature has the power to fix rates, the Court decided in 1876, the question of whether rates are reasonable or not is a legislative, not a judicial, matter. But not, said the Court of 1890 to the Court of 1876, if the rates are so unreasonable as to be confiscatory. Then it may be a matter for judicial review.

Should telephone rates be based on the general price level as it shifts from year to year, or on a price level of some years back? A public service commission, said the Supreme Court to the Maryland commission in 1935, cannot base rates on a shifting price level. But a state tax board, the Court said on February 3, 1936, when taxing railroads must take into consideration reduced values caused by economic depression.

But of all such instances of veering interpretation, the "rule of reason" in the Sherman Act cases is

* But, said the Court in its amazing decision of June 1, 1936, after the above was written, New York may not regulate the wages of women who work in laundries.

perhaps the most famous. This act, passed in 1890, made illegal "EVERY contract, combination in the form of trust or otherwise, or conspiracy in restraint of trade or commerce among the several States." In the Sugar Trust case in 1895 the Court admitted the existence of a monopoly, but said nothing could be done about it by the Federal Government without invading the reserved rights of the States.

Frontal attacks of monopolies on the Sherman Act, however, were not immediately successful. Big business first tried to get Congress to amend the act by having it apply only to "unreasonable" restraints on trade. That endeavor failing, corporation lawyers turned to the courts. What Congress refused to do, the Supreme Court did in 1911 when cases involving the Standard Oil Company and the American Tobacco Company were before it. The Court said the Sherman Act applied only to "unreasonable" restraints of trade. Justice Harlan, in a powerful dissent, pointed out that in the Trans-Missouri case only a few years before the Court had said that to insert the word "unreasonable" in the Sherman Act would be "judicial legislation" on its part.

* * *

Those who agree with a given decision of the Court frequently say to those who disagree with it: "If you don't like the way the Court interprets the Constitution, why don't you amend the Constitution?"

That has been done in the past, and doubtless will

be done again in the future. Certainly we should look upon the amending mechanism as an integral part of the Constitution, as the framers conceived it, to be used frankly and naturally whenever sufficient need arises. There is, however, much more to the problem than that.

For one thing, consider the attitude of a Marshall towards the Constitution as contrasted with the attitude of a Taney. To Taney the Constitution apparently was a rigid set of rules within a steel frame, inorganic, static, fixed for all time. To Marshall such a view of the Constitution would have seemed incredible. It would make a "more perfect Union" in a changing world impossible. Marshall was positive that was not the view of the Constitution taken by the men who framed it, most of whom he knew. The Constitution, he believed, was intended to endure for ages. It followed as surely as day follows night that, in order to endure, the Constitution simply had to be adapted to the various crises of human affairs. Isn't it therefore at least possible that the responsibility for a controverted decision rests on the Court quite as much as on the Constitution? If that is so, proposals to amend the Constitution may often be naïve and even futile.

In the second place, it can never be forgotten that several of the most important powers conferred upon Congress by the Constitution were conferred in language so broad as to be almost all-inclusive. If it were desired to give Congress more power over commerce, how could language be broader than that Congress shall have power "To regulate commerce ... among the several States?" If it were desired to give the Federal Government sufficient power to tax and spend to promote the general welfare, however that welfare may change from generation to generation, what language should be chosen in place of the words, "The Congress shall have power to lay and collect taxes ... to pay the debts and provide for the ... general welfare of the United States?"

Perhaps many of the Supreme Court's own decisions have come between it and the Constitution. Perhaps the Court has sometimes been swayed by the economic and social philosophies of its members. Still, it has also changed with the changes in the trend of the times. And from time to time various members of the Court have been far more conscious than the layman of the perils of judicial legislation, as in the invention of the "rule of reason," and judicial amendment, as in modern interpretations of the tenth amendment.

Most Americans do want government to assure as much stability as is compatible with the modern world. That is true whether their incomes are a thousand or a million dollars a year. Many times the Court has provided that stability. And many times the Court has protected the helpless against cruel and unusual punishment, or against the loss of those inalienable rights of man.

But contemporary questions about the Court, the

Constitution, and the whole judicial process involve economic matters more than any other. There always is, in economic matters, an appropriate time for change. Owners of concentrated wealth and economic power usually refuse to admit this. The Court has also frequently refused to admit it in time to effect the change smoothly and without grievous distress. When the Court in such situations refuses to budge, the average citizen rises to inquire, "Whose Constitution is it, anyway?"

The average citizen does not raise such a question flippantly or irreverently. He has too much emotional attachment to American institutions, but when there seems to him to be a conflict between what the Constitution says and what the Supreme Court says it says, he dare not suppress his concern.

The answer to questions of this sort, it seems to me, may in part be found among the many legal devices currently suggested, but the fundamental answer can be supplied only by the Supreme Court itself. The American people have granted to the Court the supreme power which comes from admiration and reverence. The Court strengthens or weakens this great power as it serves or fails to serve the general welfare.

The American people have faith in the Supreme Court of the United States, and they desire to keep this faith. The Supreme Court, in turn, must have and keep faith in the American people and in their representative government.

Chapter XV

THE COURT OF LAST RESORT

BEYOND the Courts, the President, the Congress and even the Constitution itself stands that Court of Last Resort, the Court of Public Opinion. It is here that the General Welfare is continually being defined and expressed. It is to this Court that the agencies of education and information continually appeal.

Public Opinion has a world significance today far greater than ever before because of the world-wide scope of rapid communication and transportation. Public Opinion can now be rapidly formed and, of necessity, it must be rapidly informed in order to meet the needs of the times. The press, the radio, the motion picture and the schools have a far greater responsibility for promoting the General Welfare by means of good government than is commonly recognized. They are, in fact, as important social instruments as the President, the Congress or the Courts, and in many ways they are the most important part because they have or should have in them the element of flexibility which enables society to mold itself more successfully in the direction of the General Welfare of the future.

Among the agencies molding Public Opinion, we should perhaps expect more from the colleges and universities than any of the others. Here, if anywhere, we should find understanding of the past and openmindedness toward the future. The scientists, philosophers and economists of the universities should be so sensitized toward the oncoming future, that they can serve in the field of "social weather" a position somewhat analogous to that of our weather forecasters. If storms are in prospect, we should expect the institutions of higher learning, free from partisan bias and concerned with the long time General Welfare, to suggest the kind of storm cellars to build.

Can the universities furnish the social or economic lookouts to warn of dangers ahead or suggest that calmer passages may be found if the course is changed? Ships carry such a lookout. Why not society? It happens, of course, that there is some division of counsel among the social lookouts in the universities and that some of them discern icebergs ahead when they are not there. Nevertheless it would seem to be one of the responsibilities, from which true universities should not escape, to offer fearlessly and calmly their judgment on social and economic affairs.

Short-time public opinion is formed largely on the basis of the information furnished by the radio, newspapers and the magazines. The technique of these agencies has been enormously speeded up but the volume of rapidly changing, highly specialized knowledge has increased with even greater speed. Reporters, radio announcers and magazine writers

are asked to provide the public daily, weekly and
monthly not only with all of the pertinent facts but
to put these facts together in an interesting way so
that the relationships between them will become
clear.

Inasmuch as Public Opinion is the Court of Last
Resort, we ask that the schools, the press, the radio,
the motion pictures be reasonably free from prejudice
and bias. When any one of these agencies gravely and
persistently distorts the news or shows bitter prejudice or extreme bias, we have as much right to
be shocked as though a public official were to
prove false to his trust. We ask of the molders of
Public Opinion that there be neither sins of commission nor omission where the General Welfare is
concerned.

Arthur Hays Sulzberger, publisher of the New
York *Times*, speaking before the American Newspaper Publishers' Association meeting recently
voiced the concern of responsible newspaper men
that is felt because of certain newspaper practices
and public reactions to the press when he said:

. . . There is, in my opinion, a growing disposition on
the part of the public to view with skepticism that which
they read in their newspapers and to distrust newspaper
motives. I do not raise the question as to whether that
criticism is just or unjust; I make no attempt to fathom
its depth or measure its extent. The important thing is
that it exists. The essential thing is to consider why it
exists. Three reasons impress me immediately.

In the first place, I detect certain doubts as to the accuracy of reporting. We know that our news coverage is more complete and more carefully checked than ever before. But isn't there too great a striving for color at the sacrifice of fact? Isn't the rewrite man allowed too great a degree of latitude?

In the effort to "interpret" the news, aren't we permitting too much opinion to creep into our news columns, rather than holding them unrelentingly to news and background? Are not the press associations too free in the manner in which their home offices "freshen up" a morning story for an evening service, and vice versa?

... Second, there is discernible a feeling among a considerable group of readers that the personal interests of publishers are often put ahead of public service.

... And, finally, I should say that the failure to keep editorial opinion out of the news columns, and closely akin to it, the failure to present adequately both sides of a moot question, are matters of growing concern. This indictment is made most sharply, of course, in these election days; but with the increasing complexities in industrial relations, and for that matter with the growing debate over the very structure of capitalism, it is a test that confronts us almost constantly.

The difficulty confronting the newspaper, the radio station or the motion picture producer is that the informed general public demands a high degree of freedom from prejudice and bias whereas the producer of the information must, of necessity, do his best to make a profit for those who have put their money into the venture. At this point comes in the advertiser, the circulation man and those who be-

lieve that it is more important to entertain and shock
the public than to inform it. Advertisers have at
least an indirect influence on most agencies of public
opinion because they pay most of the money which
brings the news so cheaply to the public.

Any one who has ever been connected with a newspaper, magazine, motion picture outfit or institution
for higher education is familiar with the continual
conflict in objectives. Here we find working automatically a system of checks and balances which
tends to drive sensitive natures almost crazy.
Philosophical editors have puzzled over this situation
for generations and have learned with regard to
certain subjects to work out compromises which irk
some of them tremendously at times. The situation
is probably not as bad, however, as some sensitive
editors seem to feel, especially when we consider the
only two alternatives which seem to offer themselves. The one alternative would involve government subsidy and control such as exists in various
parts of Asia and Europe and the other would involve going to the extreme of frankly operating the
agencies of information as purely profit-making
institutions.

Some people in the United States think the latter
alternative has indeed completely triumphed. For
example, some years ago when the New York *Herald
Tribune* stated the commonly approved notion that
"the American newspaper has always been an institution affected with a public interest," the *Wall*

Street Journal of January 20, 1925, replied brusquely
as follows:

"It is flatly untrue, but there is much ignorance
and hypocrisy about the matter calling for some
plain speaking.

"A newspaper is a private enterprise, owing nothing whatever to the public, which grants it no
franchise. It is therefore 'affected' with no public
interest. It is emphatically the property of its owner
who is selling a manufactured product at his own
risk. . . . Editors, except where they own their own
newspapers, take their policy from their employers.
. . . But for ridiculously obvious reasons, there are
many newspaper owners willing enough to encourage
the public in the delusion that it is the editor of a
newspaper who dictates the selection of news and
the expression of opinion. He only does so subject to
correction and suggestion of the proprietor of the
paper, who, most properly, considers his newspaper
as a plain business proposition. It is just that, no
more and certainly no less."

Now it may be that a few newspaper publishers
have thrown over many of their ideals concerning service to the General Welfare and have become "economic men" with no purpose but to line their pockets
with money as fast as possible. But this is certainly
not true of the majority. The press on legal grounds
has protested against being regarded as primarily a
profit-making institution. On the same grounds, it
has obtained preferred postal rates from the Post

Office Department. If the press were really regarded
as the *Wall Street Journal* regarded it in 1925, the
public would undoubtedly alter its attitude toward
the right of some segments of the press to abuse their
constitutional freedom. Surely the press does not
care to stand before the public as primarily a profit-
making institution.

With regard to the other alternative, government
subsidy and control, there is very little to be said in
its favor. I doubt if one person in ten thousand in the
United States seriously would suggest government
control. No matter what kind of government we
have in the United States, there is no likelihood of it
throttling the press. The people simply would not
stand for it. They would discount the bias of a government press as they discount the bias of private publications, and would be less well served with one
dominant bias than with many. Nor does it seem,
even if the people would stand for it, that a controlled press would achieve its purpose. To be effective, it would have to possess that widespread popular interest which is the great achievement of our
press; this interest is a product of the diversified approach of many publishing enterprises and would
surely be decreased by official standardization. The
more effective field of government publications
seems to be in serving special fields, reporting
the technical and highly specialized activities that
are of first concern to limited groups.

In my opinion, not the newspapers but rather the

government and the public would turn out to be the chief losers from governmental control of the press.

The American press insofar as it remembers its loyalty to the general welfare, performs a great service to the government in searching out and exposing its weaknesses and its mistakes. This service no doubt is frequently irritating to public officials, but nevertheless it does give them incentive to avoid errors of administration, and to correct mistakes that have occurred.

The great future opportunity for the American press lies in its chance to develop and perfect its facility for constructive reporting of social and economic events, movements and trends. This opportunity calls for an independent and courageous press, understandingly informing the public about the progress of government, and of the reasons for its actions, but not hesitating to expose mistakes when mistakes are made. It calls for a press sincerely and constructively devoted to the general public welfare.

This full functioning of the press would not be possible if all newspapers were controlled by the government. A press become completely supine to the domination of government would be as useless as a press become completely supine to the domination of entrenched wealth.

It would seem, therefore, that those who work for the various agencies of public opinion will con-

tinually find themselves in the rather uncomfortable
position of trying to serve the general welfare the
greater part of the time but finding it necessary oc-
casionally to color the news for the sake of an
advertiser or to overplay the news for the sake of
increasing circulation. The danger to the press, the
radio and the movie is that it will misjudge the public
and by offending public opinion eventually reduce its
own freedom and security. It is possible for molders
of public opinion to turn public opinion against
themselves. The Washington correspondent for the
London *Times*, Sir Wilmott Lewis, addressing the
annual luncheon of the Associated Press at Washington on April 20, 1936, expressed the attitude of
many others when he said:

"... both in England and the United States the
danger which confronts what we call freedom of the
press is not chiefly from without, for that we can
meet, but from within. It is, as I see it, a danger
which grows with the growth and with the increasing
integration of the newspaper system—the danger
that the freedom which makes us great and useful
may make some among us too great, that individuals
may acquire a power which (if the freedom we demand is to be ours) they cannot be prevented from
harnessing in the service of personal ambition rather
than of the community from which their strength
flows. We are all of us, each in his place and degree,
among the guardians of freedom, but ... who shall
guard your own guards?"

Democracy and tolerance go together, Sir Wilmott observed, but so do absolutism and intolerance. Power may be the enemy of tolerance, and it matters not whether the power is possessed by men in government or outside of government. What of the power of the owner of a great chain of newspapers, or radio stations, or motion picture theaters or studios? Sir Wilmott quotes Graham Wallas to the effect that the owner of a group of papers has more absolute ir-responsibility in the use of great power than any other living man.

According to information provided by *Editor and Publisher*, daily newspapers are published in some 1,450 cities of the United States. In only 300 of these cities are truly competitive newspapers published. Of the remaining 1,150, about 900 have only one paper, and 250 have two newspapers but under common ownership.

This is a trend that has long been in existence, and apparently still is operating, for between 1920 and 1936, my informant estimates, non-competitive conditions have been created by consolidation or suspension of newspapers in some 300 cities. I do not pretend to know the answer to the problem presented by this trend, but surely it deserves the earnest attention of the press itself. Much the same problem exists, of course, in the field of radio and motion pictures, and is complicated by increasing common ownership of both newspapers and radio stations.

For the sake of healthy public opinion it would be
well if the public could know more about the indirect
influence of advertising, political bias, economic
bias and other types of bias, on the writing of headlines, the presentation of news and the statement of
editorial policy. Inasmuch as all of us, even the most
abstract scientists, are subject to bias and inasmuch
as all agencies of public opinion of necessity are subject to an enormous amount of bias, there is no
reason whatever to be shocked at the discovery of
any particular bias. Nevertheless if the public is to
make up its mind in a way which insures safety for
the general welfare in the long run, it is important
that more of us should know about the types of
prejudice which are coloring the presentation of
public information at the source.

It is easy for crusaders to hold up their hands in
horror at the press of the United States. But compared with the press of many countries abroad, it
seems to me that the United States press as a whole
is remarkably impartial and competent. The high
quality of an increasing amount of news and com-
ment now going out of Washington indicates that a
finer and higher type of American journalism may
be rapidly developing. A good many reporters seem
to have the will and the skill to dig deep into economic and social realities, taking genuine interest in
them and dramatizing the march of ideas, events
and causes. It seems to me that in this respect the
press is performing an immense and growing public

service. Many of our great newspapers now cover
the news, political and otherwise, in a manner that
is as free from partisanship as one has a right to
expect in this imperfect world. Moreover many of
our newspapers have high standards of decency, as
well as of accuracy.

Many of our newspapers, but not all. Unfortunately, there are a few newspapers and other
agencies of information which abuse their constitutional freedom and endeavor to distort public opinion both by sins of commission and omission. It is
these agencies which make it so difficult for the
majority of reputable and public-minded publishers
to preserve their freedom, their power and their
opportunity to serve the general welfare.

This minority not only perverts the truth on the
editorial page, in the news and in the headlines, but
also promotes shallow thinking of a sort which opens
the nation to adopting hastily policies which are
definitely harmful to the general welfare. For example, it is easy in these days to create a strong feeling against foreign nations, and, therefore, a feeling
that imports from foreign countries, whether needed
or not, are terrible. There is no recognition of the
fact that if we do not import we cannot long export
and that therefore moderate imports of the right kind
of things are essential to keep employed those people
engaged in producing, handling and transporting
our huge volume of exports. Newspapers which use
the sacred appeal to patriotism to stir up passions

which set section against section and which harm
the general welfare are endangering themselves, the
newspaper fraternity as a whole, and the nation.
Such abuses of freedom of the press are serious, but
fortunately the public has a way of protecting itself.
Eventually there is a reaction against newspapers
which persistently color the news. In certain of our
cities the prejudices of the chief newspapers become
so well known that the majority of readers continually discount the information which they receive,
and therefore in the world of practical affairs take the
opposite position to that taken by the newspapers.

There is an interesting readjustment going on at
the present time between newspapers and public
opinion. I am referring now to the newspapers which
make a definite effort to be as fair and unbiased as
possible. Most of these newspapers, as well as the
others, are somewhat reactionary from the standpoint of economic policy. That the public is less reactionary at the present time than most of the newspapers, in indicated by the votes taken by various
private polling agencies, notably the Institute of
Public Opinion. This agency which has been conducted in co-operation with certain of the newspapers, has employed what seems to be a somewhat
scientific method of sampling and taking its votes.
This is shown by the vote on the Triple-A, for instance, which was announced by the Institute the
day before the Supreme Court decision. Only 23 percent of the population of the United States lives on

farms and probably less than 25 percent of the great newspapers supported the Triple-A. Nevertheless, the vote as announced by the Institute of Public Opinion indicated that 41 percent of the people of the United States were in favor of it. How did it happen that so many people in the United States were in favor of the Triple-A when only 23 percent are farmers and the majority of the newspapers were against the Triple-A? The same situation existed in an even more pronounced form with respect to the vote on States rights versus centralized government. For the moment the editorial policy of most of the newspapers seems to be against the government in Washington. In the poll, however, 56 percent of the people expressed themselves in favor of meeting national problems in a national way. In the South, especially, the people voted for less States rights rather than more States rights. Of course, it is worth while to have a healthy skepticism concerning all polls of public opinion because the questions are so often loaded in a manner to provoke the answer desired. In so far as the Institute of Public Opinion has a bias, however, it would seem to be on the side of conservatism rather than of liberalism, and I would guess that these particular votes are probably unbiased either by the form of the question or by the method of obtaining the votes. From this and other evidence it would seem rather clear that public opinion is oftentimes remarkably independent of the points of view fostered by a majority of the newspapers.

One of the most potent ways of forming public opinion is by face-to-face contact. In the old days this function was served by lyceums and farmers' institutes. Nowadays we have forums and discussion groups. Some one gives a lecture for three-quarters of an hour on one of the debatable economic questions of the day, then there are questions and answers for another three-quarters of an hour. By this method it is possible to measure the sincerity of any one who stands decidedly for any particular point of view. This method of developing public opinion in some ways is the best of all because there is something electric about the contact which takes place in a discussion group which brings into being an understanding of the various elements of the problem such as no one person in the group, not even the lecturer, had before the discussion began.

Beyond the government and beyond all the agencies of public opinion there stands in a democracy as a court of last resort, the people themselves. If this court is to make enlightened judgment, it must have free access to all of the facts. There rests, therefore, a tremendous responsibility on the agencies of information which bring facts to the people. The newspapers, the radio, and all the rest, from the standpoint of their own long-time welfare, as well as the national welfare, must do their best to keep clear the stream of information which flows through their channels. Of necessity there must be wide divergence of opinion in the editorial columns as to what con-

stitutes the general welfare. There is every reason
why there should be conservative, liberal and radical
points of view. Analysts of all shades of opinion
render a valuable service to the public in stating just
what they believe. But with regard to the facts
themselves, the public has a right to demand that
there be no partisan coloring. If the agencies of
public opinion play the public false in this respect,
both our democracy and the freedom of the press will
fall into real danger.

The court of last resort must ask of every one who
appears before it: "What is your prejudice? Tell me
before I begin to read or listen to you. Perhaps you
don't know you have a prejudice. In that case I am
going to discover your particular one for myself."
Yes it is right that the public should always have a
skeptical attitude because no one is free from bias.
Neither lawyers, nor judges, nor scientists, nor university professors are entirely free from personal
opinion or factional bias. We are all colored by the
place where we were born, the politics of our fathers,
the way in which we are now living, the religious
training of our mothers, and the prospects of the
future.

The advantage of vesting final judgment in all the
people themselves, as the court of last resort, lies in
the fact that if the agencies of public opinion deal
with the people honestly, they will form a judgment
on behalf of the general welfare. The people as a
whole, of necessity, cancel out the special interests

and discount the special pleaders once they stand revealed. The will of the majority must in the end be taken as the best approximation to a merging of interests in the general welfare. This means that the few who stand at points of special vantage, such as in the great universities or the newspaper offices, or the broadcasting rooms, should feel themselves engaged in a very peculiar and unusual way in serving the general welfare in the long run. They are preserving democracy and cannot betray it to special interests without grave peril, both to democracy and to themselves.

Part Four
DEMOCRACY IN ACTION

Chapter XVI

NATIONAL PROBLEMS NATIONALLY
SOLVED

In THE early days of the nation when economic units were nearly all small and local, the nature of Federal power was a simple thing. The activities of 90 percent of the people were agricultural in nature or conducted in connection with agricultural communities. Laboring men who had no jobs or who didn't like their wages started to work at farming. The job of the Federal Government was to promulgate rather simple rules of the game having to do with tariffs, money, national defense, the method of laying taxes and the method of enforcing contracts. As long as there was plenty of cheap land, shifting of population to the West, and a feeling of great growth, progress and rising values, there was not much concern on the part of the national government or the local governments with such matters as the regulation of hours and wages of labor, agricultural production, conservation of soil fertility, unemployment insurance, governmental promotion of decent housing or the regulation of prices and competitive conditions.

But when 90 percent of manufacturing industry and 50 percent of the population moved into the cities and were largely under the control of the

corporate form of organization, the Federal attitude
toward industry, agriculture and labor, of necessity
changed. Perhaps it would be more accurate to say
that the attitude *should have* changed. Actually
there has not been as much of a change in the attitude
of the Federal Government toward its economic responsibilities as should have taken place, in view of
the extraordinary transformation in the economic
world. Inventions of new methods of manufacturing,
transportation and communication have been accompanied first by inventions in corporation technique,
and later by inventions in the technique of labor and
agricultural organization. These mechanical inventions and economic powers manifested themselves
on a continent-wide scale with greater facility in
1936 than did the corresponding powers 150 years
ago on a State-wide scale.

The Federal Government started out in the United
States by being concerned chiefly with the co-ordination of political powers. Its concern with the co-
ordination of economic activity and economic powers
was secondary and that was chiefly through the
control of tariffs and money. As inventions multi-
plied, the corporations were able to utilize the
Federal power of tariff and money to unusually good
advantage. By campaign contributions and by lobby-
ing they were able to have a very definite effect every
time a tariff bill came up for consideration. As a
matter of fact, many corporations affected by tariffs
feel they have no other choice than to contribute to
both parties so that they may protect themselves in

case of need. Most corporation lobbyists in Washington no doubt feel entirely high-minded as they move from hotel room to committee room and thence to executive office trying to influence the course of legislation or of executive action. For many years a number of corporations have taken it as a matter of course that their representatives should sit more or less continuously in Washington endeavoring to shape the rules of the game so they may be as favorable as possible to the particular group which is paying the bills.

It would be amusing if it were not tragic to observe the way in which so many of the guardians of the capitalistic form of organization urge the Federal Government to keep hands off business, while at the same time they are begging for special privileges from the Federal Government in the way of tariffs, loans, subsidies and legislation designed to enable them to profit at the expense of the other classes of society. The eagerness of industry to utilize loans under RFC is a case in point. Another case is the way in which industry rushed in to utilize the Federal powers of NRA to restrict production and increase prices. It is not suggested here, of course, that all of these efforts on the part of business to utilize Federal powers are bad, but it is suggested that when industry criticizes the Federal Government for interfering with business, it is not being altogether frank. What it really means is, "Help us, don't interfere with us, and don't help the other fellow."

The significant economic development thus far

in the twentieth century is the increasing power of
the machine and the great corporation with the ac-
companying failure of political and economic organization to keep pace. But from now on it is
inevitable that there should be great strides on the
part of both labor and agricultural organizations.
Both labor and agriculture have been able to get
control in recent years of a considerable amount of
Federal power. There is no assurance as yet that
either group will have any greater respect for the
general welfare than has been the case with industry.

The Warfare of the Parts on the Whole

We now have precipitated the warfare of the parts
on the whole. The paid secretaries of the industrial,
labor and agricultural groups descend on Washington with increasing frequency.* Industry demands
higher tariffs, special subsidies, and legislation of a
type that will enable it to deal satisfactorily with
labor. Labor wants higher wages, shorter hours, unemployment insurance and the right of collective
bargaining. Farmers want higher prices and lower

* If all economic groups and interests were in a position to bring equal
pressure upon Washington through their lobbies, "government by pressure groups" might result in a fair sort of economic balance. But many
groups, such as consumers, the unemployed, small merchants and many
sections of labor, farmers and agricultural workers are poorly organized
or not at all, and even if organized they lack the money to finance powerful lobbies. Effective leverage on Washington is therefore very unevenly
applied. The pressure technique, unfortunately for people with slim
pocketbooks, boils down largely to a question of railroad fare.

interest rates, and some of them want higher tariffs. Many of the efforts of the three great groups tend to be self-defeating and to make for the general ill-fare rather than the general welfare. There is no group with adequate power whose business it is to speak and act for the general welfare. The general welfare has no paid secretaries to bring pressure in its behalf. When a Cabinet officer spoke in 1934 before the House Ways and Means Committee on behalf of lower tariffs favoring the general welfare, a Congressman from an industrial district most plaintively said:

I am here as the representative of a certain area and you, as the Secretary, of course, are the representative of the whole country; but you ought to look at the picture from the viewpoint of a congressional member, a little bit.

Most Congressmen, of necessity, have to serve their constituents. Most of them, therefore, feel that their interest in a particular class or region must be greater than their interest in the welfare of the entire United States, although, of course, many of them rationalize their position by the thought that if their class or region prospers, the whole United States will therefore also prosper. Sometimes this is true but just as often governmental efforts on behalf of a particular region or class turn out to be a positive damage to the general welfare, and very often in the long run the particular region or class is also harmed.

The harmful effects from the results of special pressure groups does not mean that the Federal Government should not concern itself with economic problems. On the contrary it may mean that the Federal Government should take a much stronger part than it has hitherto in promulgating rules of the game which serve to bring about a balance between the classes in line with the interest of the general welfare. Everybody knows that with conditions as they exist in the twentieth century, and especially as they have existed since the World War, it is impossible to bring about that balanced situation which promotes the general welfare simply by letting natural forces have their own way.

In the late eighteenth and early nineteenth centuries the people who established modern democracy were strongly in favor of the government keeping hands off because they had seen the terrible results of the governmental interferences as practiced by absolute monarchies of Europe. But that healthy democratic reaction as it found expression in France, England and the United States, finally resulted in power being appropriated, especially in England and the United States, by the wealthy, corporate interests. The powerful corporations steadily increased in power and were more and more substituted for the power of an aristocracy, though no one could say just who controlled them. The labor and farm organizations also increased steadily in power, and no one could say just who controlled them either. Each group was more or less suspicious of the other two groups, but each group was also willing to co-operate on occasion with either of the other two groups in order to put through a pet proposal. Popular impression to the contrary, it is almost certainly true that no group ever consciously acted against the general welfare. On the contrary, each group believes that its actions, by benefiting itself, are probably also benefiting the general welfare. Unfortunately, the leaders of these special groups are often so ignorant of the problems of other classes and of the general welfare that it is impossible for them to form an accurate judgment.

Federal Responsibility

The Federal Government has in effect become responsible for many aspects of our economic life whether by conscious intention or not. Thus in the case of agriculture it long sponsored a policy of stimulation, through liberal homestead laws, through irrigation projects, through scientific development, and during the war, through other legislative encouragement. In keeping with these policies, some 50 million acres were added to cultivation which later, because of the Federal high-tariff policy in conjunction with the fact that we had become a creditor nation, were no longer needed. The Federal Government, having been in considerable measure responsible for creation of the agricultural problem, could not logically side-step efforts to bring about solution of it.

The Federal Government is inevitably involved in

other aspects of our economic life. While State
governments give corporations their charters, the
present set-up of the nation's economic system is
such that most of the great corporations operate in
interstate commerce. Thus they cannot be regulated
by the States, and if their regulation is desirable, the
responsibility is the Federal Government's. When
corporations, through the powers given them, are
able in considerable measure to control prices, production and employment, the results of their policies
greatly affect the general welfare and therefore concern the Federal Government. Farmers and workers
must buy in a corporation market. Farmers must also
sell their products in a corporation market, and
laborers must sell their labor in a corporation market.
Farmers and labor have developed co-operative organizations which to some extent offset corporation
advantages, but only partially. Labor cannot protect
itself from unemployment, nor farmers by themselves match the tariff and price-control advantages
of corporations, at least not without borrowing
greater powers from government than they have
been able to do successfully so far. Finally, the
Federal Government must assume responsibility for
support of people thrown out of work by corporations
and must establish various types of social insurance.
Clearly it is not logical that the Federal Government
must shoulder the effects of powers granted by it,
without assuming more responsibility for the powers
themselves. Nor is it logical that the government put

out one set of rules for corporations and bankers and entirely another set for farmers and laboring men. There must be some unifying principle of balance in terms of the general welfare.

The Need for a Co-ordinating Mechanism

The outstanding need seems to be for a democratic mechanism which can direct action in behalf of the general welfare. There is no reason to believe that organized farmers or organized labor will in the long run act more generously on behalf of the general welfare than organized business. Each group thinks that it has a more enlightened attitude than the other, but actually the difference is probably not great. The unfortunate thing is that the various fields of activity have become so specialized that it is practically impossible for one active in the farm movement to think satisfactorily in terms of labor union language. Labor leaders may have a splendid sympathy for the agricultural problem, but as a rule it seems almost impossible for them to understand it in detail. Forward-looking business men may express sympathy for both agriculture and labor, but they are so trained in terms of profit for business that as a rule they find it impossible to think of agriculture and labor except in terms of the contribution they can make to business prosperity. Business prosperity unfortunately is not synonymous with the general welfare. Neither is agricultural nor labor prosperity.

Each group, of course, thinks that it is all-important and that if it is prosperous the others will be prosperous as well. To a certain extent this is true. For example, the profits of business, the payrolls of labor and the income of agriculture go up and down in sympathetic fashion. Nevertheless, during the decade of the '20s we had a situation when the profits of business were continuously greater proportionately than the profits of agriculture. This situation continued so long that many industrial statisticians evolved the theory that business could indefinitely be prosperous even though agriculture were going down hill. The relationship between the payrolls of labor and the income of agriculture is somewhat closer than is the relationship between business profits and farm or labor income. There are some who would like to produce general prosperity by using Federal power to make one of the three classes prosperous in the hope that prosperity in the other two classes would therefore automatically follow. Laboring men say, for example: "Increase the payrolls and the farmer's prosperity will increase because we will pay more for food." Farmers say: "Give farmers increased income and payrolls and business profits will increase automatically because we always spend our money for manufactured products." Business men say: "Let us make profits and we will promptly put laboring men to work and their increased payrolls will promptly lift the farmer out of the trough."

There is partial truth in the special pleading of each of these three groups, but I doubt if the problem of increasing the general welfare can be approached from the point of view of any one of them alone. The accident of the United States suddenly becoming a creditor nation after the World War gave the problem of lost markets for export agriculture an extraordinary importance which still continues. Nevertheless, from a long-run point of view, it is questionable whether any one group is more fundamental than the other. Each group is essential and each must subdue its intense class-consciousness to the concept of the general welfare.

In the field of government our Constitution gives us three co-ordinate branches so that each may serve as a check to the other. This system of checks has not always allowed positive action in behalf of the general welfare, but we value the balance of powers that it does give. So in the field of economic democracy, the devices we must eventually create will need to give balanced powers to economic groups: to labor, capital, farmers and consumers. In establishing such devices, it will be necessary in the first place to bring up to equality the powers and voice of some groups now not adequately recognized. At present, large segments of labor, agriculture, and consumers are without voice in our economic affairs.

Every group, however, which obtains special governmental powers such as the tariff, legal devices such as the corporate form of organization, or a governmental subsidy such as the farmers have under the new soil conservation act, or special consideration such as labor has under the Guffey Act* or the Wagner Labor Relations Act, should be required to recognize the claims of the general welfare. It happens that in the soil conservation act the welfare of the consumer is recognized in a special consumer clause providing that after due allowances are made for loss of export markets the same quantity of stuff should be available for domestic consumers per capita as in the decade of the '20s. In most class legislation, however, there is not sufficient recognition of the rights of the consumer and the general welfare. But even though all past class legislation and all future class legislation should have written into it special consumer and general welfare protection, we can't help questioning whether the situation is well taken care of. The general welfare should be promoted not merely by negative proposals written in terms of limitations on class legislation. In addition there should be a positive mechanism of some sort to promote the general welfare.

On several occasions I have suggested that sooner or later there should be a council for the general welfare. The Supreme Court has stated that it has no legal function in dealing with matters of economic policy. For example, in the Schechter decision the Court said, "It is not the province of the Court to consider the economic advantages or disadvantages of such a centralized system." Again in 1934 in the

* The Guffey Act was declared unconstitutional after this was written.

Nebbia case, the Supreme Court, referring to the right of a State to adopt a given economic policy designed to promote the general welfare, said, "The Courts are without authority either to declare such policy, or, when it is declared by the legislature, to override it." Again in the famous Northern Securities case, the Court said, "Whether the free operation of the normal laws of competition is a wise and wholesome rule portrayed in commerce is an economic question which this Court need not consider or determine."

Inasmuch as the courts feel they have not been given the power to deal with economic problems in economic terms and inasmuch as most Congressmen feel they must of necessity represent their constituency rather than the general welfare, it would seem that there is real need for some type of mechanism to reconcile the warring pressure groups. Probably a council for the general welfare should not be started in too ambitious a fashion, but if it were composed of high caliber men capable of commanding the respect of labor, agriculture and industry, as well as the reputable citizens of various political faiths, it would seem that a council of this sort might be of use in advising the Congress with respect to those of its enactments which have economic significance. It might be the duty of such a council to give its mature judgment to the legislative, executive and judicial branches of the Government as to the economic significance of pending legislation. In the first instance, a council for the general welfare might have no powers other than advisory. Later on it might be worth while to give such a council a mechanism for referring certain matters of fundamental economic concern directly to the people after an opportunity had been given for presenting all sides of such issues to the public.

If we are to have people thinking more continuously and effectively of the general welfare, it would seem to be necessary not merely to have a council for the general welfare in the Federal Government but also to have either committees for the general welfare or consumer co-operative organizations all over the country. No one yet knows what the fully expressed will of the American people will be to the myriad pressures of the special interest groups at Washington. It would seem, however, that there would be increasing discussion of the necessity of a mechanism for expressing the general welfare as opposed to the special interests. Our government of checks and balances perhaps too much favors the special interests. On the other hand, if a mechanism for the general welfare is too much emphasized, there is perhaps some danger of developing a type of non-democratic totalitarian or corporative state which we do not desire. We wish to retain our democratic processes but we want to cleanse them from the over-influence of the special pressure groups. We wish to discover policies which will work in the long run for the general interest and which are so meritorious that they will be accepted by all reasonable people and parties.

Chapter XVII

FOR THE LONG PULL

OUR failure to develop an agricultural, industrial and foreign trade policy during the 1920's which would add up to make sense in the 1930's brought us into the pit of depression in 1932. In this situation, emergency rather than long-time programs were inevitable. Factory workers out of jobs, farmers in process of being dispossessed of their farms, incipient revolt among these injured classes, no signs of the speedy lifting of the depression: these circumstances called for quick and stop-gap action in 1933. They called for relief to the unemployed, relief to industries and individuals struggling under a tremendous weight of debt, relief to farmers whose prices and income were smashed under towering surpluses.

We need to gird ourselves now for the long pull in agriculture and industry. Real gains have been made in coming out of the awful emergency of 1932 and some of our experiences are beginning to point the way to programs that will make sense in terms of decades instead of emergencies. This is particularly true of the agricultural programs that are now being developed with a view toward the long-time needs of agriculture and the nation. Most of this chapter is devoted to our agricultural experiences in going from emergency programs toward the more basic adjustments, but they serve also to suggest the broad lines along which the economic democracy of the future, embracing agriculture, industry, and distribution, must be directed.

The agricultural adjustment programs of 1933 and 1934 were adopted under this emergency pressure. In the previous four years, farmers had seen their farm prices fall from an average of 45 percent above the 1913 level to 45 percent below. In 1932, their gross farm income had slumped to half what it was four years before, but interest, taxes and railroad rates had stayed about the same. The farmer's dollar could buy only 60 cents worth of industrial goods as compared with 1913. The value of his land was 30 percent under the prewar value, but his mortgage debt was twice as great.

The loss of foreign trade plus city unemployment piled up the tremendous farm surpluses which were the immediate cause of the farmer's desperate situation. Prices smashed to a third the 1929 level could not move these surpluses into either foreign or domestic markets. Granaries and warehouses were swamped with three times the normal carryover of wheat and cotton, while stocks of corn, hogs and tobacco were far above normal. The same surpluses were partly responsible for bread-lines in the cities; impoverishing farmers, they destroyed hundreds of thousands of jobs dependent on farmers' buying power. It was a vicious and descending spiral.

The Emergency A.A.A. Program

Farm leaders, unable to deal directly with city un-employment or to restore foreign markets, could at least conceive a program to deal with the farm sur-pluses which would improve not only the farm situation but the industrial situation as well. Bring-ing down the unsalable surpluses to normal levels, without reducing supplies needed for domestic con-sumption or available exports, could bring about a recovery of farm prices, increase farmers' incomes and thus restore city jobs dependent on farmers' purchasing power. By halting the deflation of com-modity and land values, confidence in the credit structure in general could be greatly strengthened. A lift to the sagging weight of farm distress might help move the whole economic machine off "dead center" and start it turning toward recovery.

These immediate objectives for agriculture had to be aimed not at the whole farm problem in its long-time aspects, but at the worst emergency phases. These had to do particularly with the situation of farmers who produce our chief exports: cotton, to-bacco, wheat and hog products. Producers of these commodities had been worst hit by the loss of foreign trade, and it was in the regions where these export products are grown that the effective purchasing power for the products of some 50 million acres of land had been lost.

With the assistance of the State Agricultural Colleges, the Extension Service, and 3 million co-operating farmers working through State and county committees, the emergency program got under way with surprising speed and efficiency in view of the fact that completely new social machinery had to be set up. Unusually bad growing weather in 1933, 1934 and 1935 hastened the reduction of surpluses, and other phases of the recovery program with the AAA, aided in the improvement of the farm situation. The results may be summarized briefly as follows:

Farmers reduced their acreage of export crops by 36 million acres in 1934 and 30 million acres in 1935.

Surpluses of wheat and hog products moved into consumption and were practically normal by the end of 1935; surpluses of cotton and tobacco were greatly reduced and were approaching normal.

Farm prices rose from 52 percent of the prewar level in December, 1932, to 110 percent in December, 1935, an improvement of 111 percent. The farmer's dollar, which could buy 60 cents worth of other goods in 1932, could buy 86 cents worth in 1935.

Cash farm income rose from $4,377,000,000 in 1932 to $6,276,000,000 in 1934, and approximately $6,900,000,000 in 1935, a total increase of 60 percent.

Farmers increased their purchases of goods from $3,900,000,000 in 1932 to $6,700,000,000 in 1935, or an increase of 70 percent. About 40 percent of the workers re-employed in industry between 1932 and 1935 owed their jobs to this increase of nearly 3 billion dollars in farmers' buying power.

In spite of the increase in farm prices and limited industrial recovery, factory workers in 1935 paid

no greater proportion of their income for food than
they had paid in 1928. Factory workers who had
received 60 percent of their 1928 income in 1933,
received 80 percent of the 1928 income in 1935.
Their food cost them 80 percent as much as it did
in 1928.

The farmer's position was also improved by lower
interest rates on debts re-financed by the Farm
Credit Administration, by lower taxes, and by other
programs which enabled them to increase the share
of cash receipts available for purchase of city
products.

Only the supply of some meat products, due to the
extreme drought of 1934, was somewhat below a
normal level in 1935. In the case of other major
commodities, a relatively healthy balance had been
restored between supplies and markets. Farm income
in 1935 was better distributed as between the several
agricultural regions than it had been in the preceding five years, and farm and city income was in
better relationship. Two major difficulties, however,
stood in the way of general recovery for agriculture
as well as industry. One was the persistent decline
in foreign demand; the other was the inability of
industry to increase activity to the point where the
unemployed and those on relief could be given jobs.

What We Learned from A.A.A.

The emergency acreage control programs in cotton, wheat, corn, hogs and tobacco gave us some-

thing more than a contribution to improved farm
income and a healthier balance between farm and
city buying power. There were by-products of considerable importance in long-range planning for
agriculture and industry. In the first place we
learned that, given definite objectives, and given a
Congress and Administration willing to recognize the
reasonable economic motives of producers and to
supply the necessary centralizing power of government, millions of farmers stand ready to enter into a
co-operative venture, and through their local committees and individual referenda to pave the way
toward economic democracy. In the second place,
as the agricultural adjustment programs and nature
reduced the surpluses, it was possible to turn attention to more permanent types of agricultural adjustment; and third, as the basic features of a long-time
farm program came into view, they served to emphasize as well the basic features of a long-time
industrial program.

In early 1935, nearly a year before the Supreme
Court destroyed the emergency production control
programs, we started an inquiry among the State
Experiment Stations as to the best types of farming
to conserve the soil in each region. State and regional
groups were organized to utilize the best technical
information in determining how best to shift from
the AAA type of control programs to programs that
would not only maintain the gains and the balances
achieved, but also be more scientifically adapted to

the needs of regions and individual farms. Instead of surpluses, the phenomena of postwar industrial depressions, we were turning our attention to the more persistent problems such as soil erosion, the maintenance of soil fertility, and other aspects of a sound national land-use policy. Sound progress in this direction could not be very rapid, partly because an immediate shifting from direct commodity acreage control programs year by year to long-time programs that overlooked the short-time possibilities would expose agriculture to a new cycle of surpluses.

The spectacular recovery in wheat, cotton, tobacco and hogs during 1933–1935 could be whittled away by normal weather in 1936 and 1937, especially if export markets continued unable to take our surpluses and if industrial activity continued below its 1929 level. Under the Agricultural Adjustment Act of 1933 and 1935 we were proceeding in an orderly fashion to lay the necessary progressive bridges between the short-time emergency control programs and the long-time land-use programs. However, as a result of the Supreme Court action of January 6, 1936, we are launched on a soil conservation program in 1936, probably two years sooner than sound planning would call for.

Shifting to a Long-Time Soil Program—in a Hurry

When the production control program was destroyed by the Supreme Court, we at once made arrangements to call in representatives of the farm organizations for consultation as to a new program. Within two months a new program designed to shift acres from soil-depleting crops to soil-conserving crops was worked out by Congress, passed, and signed by the President. Farmers in four great regional meetings were called on for their advice as to the best way to put the new program into effect, and as a result of their recommendations for 1936 an effort will be made to shift about 30 million acres from soil-depleting to soil-conserving crops. The new program is a soil conservation program, but as a by-product it does some of the economic things which the old program did.

The new program pays farmers for taking land out of soil-destroying crops and putting it into soil-conserving crops. Wheat, corn, cotton and tobacco, are four of the leading soil-depleting crops. The producers of these four crops however, will not receive quite as much money for their work under the new program as they did under the old. Producers in the East and Far West will receive somewhat more. It is not possible under the new program to work so directly to improve the situation with respect to a given commodity of which there is great overproduction. The emphasis is on the soil fertility problem rather than on the commodity supply problem. Probably there will be a number of farmers in the fall of 1936 who will regret bitterly that the production phases of the agricultural adjustment program were killed by the Supreme Court action in

January of 1936. On the other hand, there will be thousands of farmers who will get along even better under the new program than they did under the old.

The new program is definitely aimed to promote the long-time general welfare of the nation. There is bound to be some confusion in the first year or two, however, because of the rapid shift that had to be made from the old to the new program. Furthermore, it remains to be seen whether the new program can enable farmers to meet the supply and demand situation during the next two or three years. Normal producing weather in 1936 and 1937 could do extraordinary things to the supplies and prices of export crops. Unless there is unusual business recovery on a world-wide basis, favorable weather could easily result in wheat at 50 cents a bushel, cotton at 7 cents a pound, hogs at $5.00 a hundred and flue-cured tobacco at 10 cents a pound.

Under the present interpretation of the Constitution by the Supreme Court, it is not possible to devise a national program which works toward both long-time and short-time objectives. In the Hoosac Mills decision, however, the Supreme Court did leave the door open for state co-operation in a program designed to meet the supply situation, and this method has been incorporated in the new Soil Conservation and Domestic Allotment Act, to be put into operation in 1938. That year should see an interesting experiment on the part of farmers in meeting their supply problem in this manner. Farm surpluses were not abolished by the Supreme Court, and farmers I think are looking forward to using the mechanism which the Court has left open to them to meet a situation upon which the Court admittedly did not rule.

I am hopeful that State co-operation may provide an efficient mechanism for dealing with the surplus problem which will very likely face farmers within a year or two if we have normal weather. It is rather ironical, however, that the farmers of the nation should need to take a roundabout way to meet a common, national problem. The National Government was conceived under the Constitution in 1787 as the people's mechanism for meeting those problems among the States which were national and not State in nature. That farmers a hundred and fifty years later would not be able to use the interstate mechanism already provided by the Constitution (that is, the Federal Government), but would need to set up a second interstate mechanism alongside the present one, is something that I believe would seem rather silly to the Founding Fathers. I believe in time we will find a way to return to the Federal mechanism as provided by the Constitution, and thus to avoid a cumbersome duplication of effort.

Meanwhile, the new AAA soil conservation program promises to be of tremendous value in working toward the long-time objective of maintaining our physical resources. The soil is our most precious

material heritage. More than 35 million acres of
cotton, corn, wheat and other intensive crops are
growing on land so subject to erosion that the result
of present cropping methods will be the loss of the
present plowed soil within a generation. Perhaps
another 100 million acres of intensive crops are
being grown under bad farming systems which
result in steady depletion of the soil fertility even
though the physical soil itself is not washing away
very rapidly. Such methods will result in the physical
basis of many communities being destroyed within
a surprisingly short time.

Agriculture can gradually be turned from a mining
industry into a true cropping industry which renews
the source of its productivity even as it yields the
needed yearly crops. Perhaps 10 percent of our farmers
are already practicing the proper methods. The
other 90 percent are not doing so, largely because
their financial circumstances will not permit. In
1936, American farmers are embarking on the most
extensive soil-renewing program ever advanced by
any government. Several million farmers will co-
operate. The new soil program may not result in
as continuous economic balance as the old AAA
program, but it will have greater long-time significance. The experience learned from the rather
hastily worked-out program of 1936 should enable
farmers, farm leaders, the Land Grant Colleges,
and government officials to develop greatly improved
methods in 1937 and the years following.

One splendid thing about both the old AAA and
the new AAA soil-conservation program is their
provision for conserving human resources as well as
soil resources. Farmers working together in community, county and State committees have learned
to feel a solidarity which they never possessed
before. The old feeling of individual helplessness has
left them. They have both information and the
ability to act. They have the essentials of economic
democracy for the first time. This they will not give
up. It is to be hoped however that as they perfect
their knowledge and power they will also learn the
virtues of due restraint so they will never impose
unduly on other classes, and so they can perfect that
balanced relationship with other classes which makes
for the general welfare.

Safe-Guarding Consumers

Another important feature of the new Soil Conservation Act is that it recognizes more directly than
did the AAA the central plank of a long-time agricultural program for the United States. The provision, that the act shall not be used to discourage
production below normal per capita domestic consumption, rests on the fact that agricultural
production, unlike industrial, has a natural limit
and therefore an easily recognized standard. That
limit is the rate of population growth. For decade
after decade the population of the United States
tends to maintain a fairly constant per capita con-

sumption of agricultural products. There have been considerable shifts in the composition of the American diet, but these have not altered noticeably the average per capita consumption of all food combined over the past 30 years. Unless our national diet changes materially in the next decade, this basic fact, coupled with the expected rate of population growth, becomes a reasonable standard for a long-time agricultural program.

It has been argued that the average per capita consumption of farm products could be materially increased, that the people of the United States have the ability to consume at home all the products of the American farms. Given no further acreage expansion and no increase in productivity per acre, the growth of population would, during the course of a decade, catch up with the present acreage. What is usually meant is that even in normal times we have low income groups whose consumption of farm products is below average and below requirements for the maintenance of health. The real problem here is the creation of a larger national income and such an equitable distribution as will lift the submerged income groups to the average level.

This means basically turning out much more in the way of industrial goods—for which there are no biological and abdominal demand limits—than is now the case. That would enable more of our population to pay the farmer a living wage for producing the more expensive foods that go with a higher income.

Fully employed and highly productive city people buy considerably more fruits and vegetables, dairy and poultry products and meats, and less of cereals. A hundred calories and a hundred units of protein in the high-quality, so-called protective foods, such as fruits, vegetables and dairy products cost several times as much as in the grains. But the grains are relatively low in vitamins, mineral matter and high-quality protein. In nine cases out of ten, when family income increases, the consumption of these protective foods also increases. These foods are relatively expensive but they are palatable and they furnish health insurance especially in the case of young children and of expectant mothers. If a corporation were running the United States from the standpoint not of profits but the national health, it would put on a tremendous agricultural adjustment program which would result in trebling the use of the so-called protective foods. Because of the increased labor required by the farmers to produce these more expensive foods, such a corporation would enable the city workers to produce more so that they might pay the farmers for their increased labors in producing these expensive foods.

Most of our families in 1929 had less than a $2,000 income. Naturally they could not buy the foods that make up the diet of, say a $3,500 family. If most of the population were now to eat and live as do those who have $3,500 incomes, our present national income would have to be doubled. This would mean doubling the production of industrial goods. But even if this miracle could be performed, it would not automatically take care of the farm problem, nor do away with the necessity of a long-time farm program. If anything, it would make the present soil and land-use program much more of a necessity, for the composition of the higher salary diet is quite different from the present one. It would call for cutting our wheat production and consumption in two and for a a marked increase in the production of fruits, vegetables, dairy, poultry and meat products. It would be necessary to make a most drastic rearrangement of our entire agricultural plant.

At the present time it seems that there is no mechanism for enabling the city workers and the city corporations to co-operate to increase the output of the right kind of goods so that the farmers can produce the increased quantities of high-quality food which the city people really need. If the farmers do their part and increase too suddenly the products which the national dietary really demands, the result may be bankruptcy to the farmers and no net gain to the city people. Apparently what is needed is a co-ordinated attack in terms of increased and more efficient production of the right kinds of goods. The farmer cannot do the job alone. It is a problem of co-operation on the part of agriculture, industry and labor, with the Federal Government helping on behalf of the general welfare.

The Long-Time Farm Problem

I do not feel that any agricultural act yet proposed is perfect or anywhere near perfect. The soil conservation program which proposes to divert some 30 million acres of soil ruining crops to soil building purposes is in some respects an improvement over the old Triple A. Nevertheless, it covers only one phase of the farm problem. Fundamentally it is impossible to build up an enduring agricultural civilization until the following three requirements have been met:

1. All farmers who work on the land must be enabled to come into ownership of the land which they work as rapidly as they have demonstrated reliability and understanding of farm management practices. There can be no abiding agricultural civilization until the same man stays on the same land for an average of at least 15 years. We need five families with a permanent interest in the land they live on for every one with such interest today.

2. The farmers must more and more own their own marketing facilities. There should be well managed co-operatives not only for selling what the farmer produces but also for purchasing his supplies. There should be co-operative financing as well as co-operative selling and purchasing. Through community co-operation they must build a satisfactory cultural life with abundant opportunity for recreation and cultural activities. Schools, churches and cultural organizations must further these ends for

the sake of the rural community itself and not merely serve as feeders for the cities.

3. The farmers through their great overhead farm organizations and through the State and Federal Governments must be prepared to see that the rules of the game as between them and the other classes are fair, and they must be prepared through these agencies to co-operate with the other classes to promote the general welfare.

A volume could be written on each of these three prerequisites to an enduring farm civilization. It is obvious that the merest beginning in realizing these prerequisites has been made in the United States. The agricultural adjustment program and the soil conservation program come under the third requisite. Practically nothing has been done in the United States to cure the rapidly growing evil of tenancy. The Bankhead Act which passed the Senate in 1935 was a definite effort in this direction. Sooner or later some bill of this sort will be passed. There must be definite effort to encourage men to own their own farms. Some method should be discovered for discouraging land speculation. Advancing land values are beneficial to the farm owner who is selling out to move to town or to California but they never were of help to the man who works his own land or to the young man who is just starting. Some way must be found to discourage excessive mortgaging as well as tenancy.

When we have thousands of communities in the

United States composed either of landowning farmers
or of tenants who are certain to be in that community
for more than five years, it will be possible to build
up a genuine co-operative spirit. As long as most of
our communities are composed of farmers who are
likely to move in three or four years, our co-operative
organizations are built more or less upon the sands.
True it is that we have a large number of very im-
posing commodity co-operatives which sell goods
very efficiently for farmers. But as long as the community co-operative spirit is not thoroughly behind
them, they are not so greatly different from such
old line business organizations as are willing to
pro-rate back part of their profits in order to retain
their customers. Most of our farm co-operatives
whether engaged in selling or in purchasing, tend to
be somewhat similar to established American business in the respective lines. Excellent work has been
done but it needs to be backed up by a more complete
co-operative philosophy in the respective communities. The Farm Credit Administration, through the
Production Credit Associations and loans to co-
operatives, makes possible farmer-controlled financing in a way that was impossible previous to 1933.

The outstanding lacks in a long-time farm program
in the United States today are first a mechanism for
enabling farmers to own the land which they work
so that there will be less shifting of farm population;
second, a more widespread appreciation of the way
in which community co-operative spirit can reinforce

the farm selling co-operatives, the farm purchasing co-operatives and the farm financing co-operatives; third, an appreciation of the farmers' duty to maintain the soil and feed the nation; and fourth, an assurance that a long-time progressively expanding industrial program, more stable than in the past, and based on such rules of the game as will promote a balanced general welfare, will give farmers a chance to contribute more abundantly to the needs of all the people.

The Long-Time Industrial Problem

The ultimate success of a long-time agricultural program depends upon the support of a progressively expanding industrial program. It is extremely unfortunate that in the early days of 1933, when the emergency contract programs were being developed for agriculture, business men were not able to develop programs with equally direct objectives for industrial production and employment. Agriculturalists saw their own problems in terms of so many acres of wheat, cotton, corn and tobacco needed for domestic use and so many not needed for the moment for export. Practically nowhere among business leaders did we have the comparable clarity of vision in terms of restoring the normal volume of production of the basic industrial products, the normal number of new homes, the normal quantity of shoes and clothing, and the normal number of men to be kept at work. Instead we had a great preoccupation with price margins, price differentials, wage rates, wage differentials and similar problems which do not get down to fundamentals. Business men preferred code authorities to restrict their already abnormally low outputs to plans for producing the things a nation in distress needed and continues to need; no real plans for determining, on the basis of the recommendations of industrial engineers and scientists, what our basic industries should produce, no mechanism for bringing together management and labor of the basic industries to determine what, in view of agreed-upon schedules of normal expanding production would be appropriate hours and wages of labor, yearly earnings, profit margins and consumer prices.

I recognize that the problem of co-operative action in the case of industry is much more difficult than in the case of agriculture, both because of the more complex organization of business and because vested rights are more powerfully concentrated in business than in agriculture. Yet this doesn't remove the need. We apparently couldn't build co-operative bridges between the basic industries, between the owners, managers and laborers in each in the interest of a common welfare. While agriculturalists were attempting to put the agricultural house in order by producing for adequate domestic consumption without the usual export surpluses, industrialists faced the necessity of developing similar programs for bringing about adequate production of industrial products, which in the case of industry meant increased industrial production. For after all, there is practically an unlimited capacity for consumption of industrial products the production of which brings employment, absorbs technological unemployment and creates our national wealth. Farm production is in a large sense intended to keep a nation properly fed and clothed that it may turn the products of the mines, quarries and factories into national wealth. Most thoughtful business men realize this basic difference, but their industrial experts have not, by and large, been called upon to consider the broad aspects of industrial and labor policy. They are as a rule paid to think in terms of what is best for the individual firm. I am certain that much progress could be accomplished toward developing a long-time, stable, expanding industrial program with appropriate inducements to capital, labor, farmers and consumers for putting it into effect, once we could bring together some of our broad-minded industrial and labor leaders to consider production schedules, payrolls, numbers of workers, fair profits, for our major basic industries as a group, and for the country as a whole.

There is practically no disagreement with the broad formula for an American industrial program. I have at times put it in the following terms:

Our national economic goal must be increased balanced production of the things which people really need and want (1) at prices low enough so consumers can buy, but high enough so producers can keep on producing, and with income so distributed that no one is shut off from participation in consumption, except those who refuse to work; (2) with scrupulous regard for the conservation of our remaining natural resources; and (3) by means characteristic of our traditional democratic processes.

So steeped have we become in our individual problems, be they those of owner, manager, labor leader, worker or consumer, that the usual reaction to this formula is the fear that it will mean a reduction in wage rates, a reduction in profit margins, a loss of individual freedom, the perpetuation of inefficient firms. Examined in the spirit of true cooperation, however, I believe this formula will be found to be an adequate basis around which to build an economic democracy to sustain and perpetuate our political democracy. We can not go on much longer having major economic depressions every decade. We must not let the present progress toward recovery divert us from the necessity of preventing the depression of the early 1940's from carrying farmers, workers and all to even lower levels of economic despair than those we touched in 1932.

Chapter XVIII

THERE IS AN AMERICAN WAY

ONE of the most fascinating things in the world is to trace the way in which ideas manifest themselves in hard physical facts and eventually in political and social machinery.* The actions of every man are based consciously or unconsciously on moral, philosophic or religious concepts which have molded

---

* While the purpose of this chapter is to stir the imagination with respect to the way in which ideas manifest themselves in the world of hard physical facts, I wish in this footnote to give recognition also to the way in which hard physical facts have a continuous effect on the world of ideas. There is a continuous back-and-forth movement between the two worlds. The philosophy of economic determinism and the materialistic dialectic of Marx gives too much credit perhaps to the physical world. Undoubtedly it must be recognized, but for the purpose of the last chapter of this book it would seem to me wise to lay the emphasis on the movement of ideas into the world of facts rather than the reverse.

Here in the United States we have a "chosen land" in which because of abundant natural resources and less pressure either of internal population or of surrounding populous nations, mankind is less compelled to travel in specific channels by hard material fact than is the case any place else in the world. We have free choice between a number of ideas. It is a matter of tremendous significance to the future of the world which type of idea we embrace. A reciprocal to this chapter might be written dealing with the natural resources of the United States and their effect on our mentality. While I recognize the desirability of such a chapter, I prefer to leave the closing emphasis in this book on the significance of the world of ideas. Man can develop a harmonious relationship between himself and the world of hard physical fact, and while in his ideas recognizing that world, he nevertheless can rise superior to it.

the traditions of the race or nation. These concepts
affect in surprising fashion the scientific, mechanical,
economic and political world. The purpose of this
chapter is to consider some of the concepts of the
past which have been formulated into social and
governmental mechanisms for the general welfare
of the United States, and then to consider some of the
possibilities for the future.

Some of the root ideas which have characterized
the people of the United States and which have
worked their way out into the world of hard physical
fact are the following:

1. Belief in democracy, liberty, freedom of speech
and the rights of man as expressed in the Declaration
of Independence and the Constitution.

2. Belief that God is best worshipped by regular
labor, frugal living, careful saving and good education for the children.

3. Belief in science, invention, mass production
and progress unlimited.

4. Belief in free competition under the rules of the
game as laid down by Adam Smith and the Manchester School of Economics.

These ideas applied by sturdy men of good ancestry in a growing country of enormous natural
resources could produce but one result—"The United
States of the early twentieth century!" Most Americans of the older stock are heartsick for the return
of the America of thirty years ago. Looking backward from the perils of the postwar period they see

that earlier, simpler America beckoning them to come back to a golden age. It will never return as it was, but it is nevertheless definitely worth while to examine the four ideas which made the America which the middle-aged people of old American stock so love.

The idea of democracy and the rights of man was widespread in both Europe and America after the middle of the eighteenth century. It seems increasingly apparent that the ideas which blossomed forth in the Declaration of Independence, the Constitution and the Bill of Rights of the United States found their English origin in the philosopher John Locke and their French origin in Montesquieu, among other philosophers of the French school. Locke in the last half of the seventeenth century developed in typically British manner the ideas of religious liberty, religious tolerance and government by the consent of the governed. The French philosophers developed in somewhat more ideal and extreme but less religious form ideas about the innate goodness of man and the probability that this goodness would manifest itself to the benefit of every one if greater freedom were permitted. The young brain trusters who wrote the Declaration of Independence and the Constitution were seriously infected with European ideas which were destined eventually to break out in the bloodshed of the French Revolution. The tremendous interest in liberty, democracy and the rights of man sprang partly from the Reformation and the Renaissance, both of which consisted largely in breaking old forms, and partly from revolt against the restrictions which more or less absolute monarchy imposed on an expanding mercantilism. Those were the days of the first encyclopedias when it was thought that all information could be compiled in books and then everybody could read everything and the knowledge and reason of man would cure all the social ills. They were grand days of faith and hope. The United States will never be able to pay her debt of gratitude to the young brain trusters who formulated these European ideas into terms of action and governmental procedure.

For the theory of checks and balances as found in our Constitution we are indebted more to Montesquieu than to any one else in Europe. Visiting England in the first half of the eighteenth century he had found that British stability had resulted from the division and balance of powers of government in England. He wrote a book on the subject entitled *The Spirit of the Laws,* and this book influenced certain members of the American Constitutional Convention. The strange thing is that the British had departed from the theory of the division and balance of powers of government before Montesquieu's book was published. At the time the constitutional Fathers read the book, the British had ceased having a departmentalized form of government such as Montesquieu extolled. Nevertheless, pressed particularly by Hamilton, the Montesquieu ideas had much to do with the formulation of the "checks and balances" theory as expressed in the Constitution. The Founding Fathers thought by the use of checks and balances they could prevent the return of any form of tyranny such as that from which they had suffered. They did not visualize the possibility that the checks and balances might conceivably promote a new tyranny of economic privilege and pressure groups and result at some distant day in the inability of the Federal and State Governments to pull together in a satisfactory manner on behalf of the national welfare.

The sixteenth, seventeenth and eighteenth century concepts about liberty, the rights of man and the innate goodness of man manifested themselves in institutions for universal education, religious toleration, universal suffrage, the direct primary and all the varied paraphernalia of democracy.* These institutions, in turn, gave an extraordinary opportunity for exploitation first by corporations and second by other organized class groups. But however much many of us may question the final outcome, all

---

* It should be mentioned in passing that many of these ideas which are supposed to characterize the Reformation, the French Revolution and American Democracy found expression in the writings of the Scholastics and their followers both before and after the Reformation. John Locke's theories of government seem to have been influenced to some extent by the English writers Hooker and Fortescue, who in turn based their reasoning on the Scholastics, who to some degree had developed a theory of the natural rights of man as opposed to the divine right of kings which was prevalent in England at the time of John Locke and immediately thereafter.

of us must admit the extraordinary vitality and power in the world of hard physical fact of the ideas which were launched by the reformers and philosophers of the sixteenth, seventeenth and eighteenth centuries. The United States is their child. The American patriots drew their inspiration from these men and gave the inspiration a body such as no one in Europe was able to do.

The Thrifty Protestant Concept

The dominant contribution of the Protestant concept in the world of affairs was a strong emphasis on the idea that the individual best worships God by regular labor, frugal living and careful saving. Men who approached God after the manner of John Knox and John Calvin found their spirits cramped in the Europe of the seventeenth century. New worlds free from the ancient bonds of church and state appealed to them. Iron men, resolute women able to bear hardship and endless toil because they thought they were carrying out God's will, laid down the outlines of a structure which made it possible to conquer a continent in record-breaking time, and always they carried their families with them, built their school houses and churches and imbued the next generation with the principles of industry and thrift.

Vital Protestantism typically found its origin with the lower middle class, but the habits of life which the Protestant idea cultivates result oftentimes in riches and thereupon a curious dilemma is presented. John Wesley recognized this when in one of his sermons he said:

I fear whenever riches have increased, the essence of religion has decreased in the same proportion. Therefore, I do not see how it is possible, in the nature of things, for any revival of true religion to continue long. For religion must necessarily produce both industry and frugality, and these cannot but produce riches. But as riches increase, so will pride, anger and love of the world in all its branches.

Wesley's only solution of the dilemma was for the rich to glorify God by giving abundantly.

Calvin had realized the difficulty and spent much labor on devising rules and regulations for the administration of property as a trust from God. But he himself lived to see the self-appointed "stewards" forget both the doctrinal source of their material "blessings" and the self-restraint in its acquisition which Calvin regarded as a direct implication of his theological ideas. Somewhat in the manner that judicial interpretation was to deny both Federal and State power to regulate modern business in the United States, the Protestant ethic, freed from the restraints of the Roman Church, failed to develop an effective discipline for the social administration of great accumulations of property. In both cases, a wide "twilight zone" was created, in which the jungle law of tooth and nail prevailed.

Many aspects of the Protestant faith no longer grip the imagination of the people of the United States as was once the case, but the great middle class, especially in the farm region, still works, denies, accumulates and trains the children of the next generation in the same spirit as always, even though the fine points of doctrine have been almost completely lost.

In the great industrial centers a curious transformation has taken place. In these areas Protestantism has become to a considerable extent identical with the upper-class way of life. The essential faith of this class is a belief in hard work, thrift, saving, the sacredness of capital, and the moral right of such a group to continue to govern, profit and reap the rewards of the good life.

The strengths and the weaknesses of the United States are undoubtedly in considerable measure the outgrowth of the fervent concepts of such men as Martin Luther, John Calvin and John Knox. Probably no mental approach to reality was better adapted to rapidly expanding wealth production than the Protestant approach. Unfortunately, it has not been quite as well adapted to wealth distribution and wealth consumption in line with the doctrines of the New Testament.

The Idea of Science and Progress Triumphant

The scientists and great inventors of the nineteenth century were, in considerable measure, a product of the emphasis laid on knowledge and the rights of man during the preceding century. The power over nature given by science and invention during the nineteenth century was so great that the idea of "Progress Unending and Unlimited" was born. This idea was not formulated in definite form by the philosophers, but it was dominant in the minds of young Americans throughout the last half of the nineteenth and the first twenty years of the twentieth century. The professors in the universities more and more accepted the material explanation of reality as the true one. Herbert Spencer, Darwin and Huxley had convinced the professors that humanity was essentially like the animals, that the animals were like the plants and that evolution starting with matter had produced life and finally humanity. The impact of scientific philosophy on Protestantism in the United States resulted in reinforcing the Old Testament aspects of Protestantism and destroying for practical purposes many of the spiritual aspects of the New Testament, thus making modern Protestantism singularly like Reform Judaism.

During the twentieth century there has been an increasing disposition to question the almightiness of science, invention and progress as holding the complete key to the good life and knowledge of the universe. Discoveries in physics, presumably the most mathematical and exact of the sciences, demonstrated that reality was much less tangible than had hitherto been supposed. The science and inventions of the nineteenth century gave man a materialistic optimism which was bound to disappear the moment the nations found it necessary to live with each other. The period of exploitation of natural resources, of labor, of agriculture and of backward people was certain to come to an end within less than a century. The illusion of the all-sufficiency of scientific invention and unlimited progress is now being demonstrated. It was a phase something like adolescence, and the United States suffered from its handicaps and benefited from its advantages more than any other part of the world. For some decades the materialistic concepts based on science will continue to dominate many of our universities. But the newer science is beginning to undermine the older science, and the United States will soon be ripe for a more adequate and fundamental philosophy.

Free Competition and Devil Take the Hindmost

Captain John Smith is reported to have said to the English adventurers at Jamestown, "If you don't work, you shall not eat." Under pioneer conditions men were stimulated to take care of themselves in a way unknown to Europe. The men of the American colonies developed the idea that they could take care of themselves and that they wanted to be left alone. This attitude which was natural in a pioneer country was reinforced, first, by the political doctrines about democracy, liberty and the rights of man, and later by the economic philosophies de-

veloped by Adam Smith and his followers. It is an
interesting coincidence that Adam Smith's *Wealth
of Nations* was published in 1776. Adam Smith
didn't like governmental restrictions, monopolies
and political control over economic affairs. He
thought it would be much simpler if free competition
would straighten out these matters instead of governmental interference. The Adam Smith views developed into a doctrine of "claw and fang" in the
economic world and for 100 years the doctrine has
been worshipped by business men. Among economists
the doctrine has increasingly been abandoned during
the past 40 years but businessmen still cling to it,
or think they do. Of course, what the businessmen
are actually clinging to is the belief that government
should interfere to give them tariffs, favorable corporation laws and monetary and taxation control
of the sort which they approve. They would be the
first to cry out in terror if the pure Adam Smith
doctrine were put into effect today. Farmers could
stand the Adam Smith doctrine put into effect
better than any one else but even they would be
tremendously harmed by a sudden application.

The idea of free competition between small business units has never been tried in the modern world.
Always there have been interferences which are much
greater than are generally appreciated by any except
those who have lived in a capital city, and have seen
the pressures applied to get government powers for
special purposes.

The significant thing about the "free competition"
ideas as they apply to American life is that by way of
the university professors they furnished a philosophy
which has been very useful to business men and
financiers in enabling them to hold on to their governmental advantages while protesting the demands
of other groups. Whenever labor and agriculture
endeavor to get anything from the government, the
professors of economics or the business men would
shout, "economically unsound," and would bring
out the familiar reasoning of classical economists.
The jargon sounded logical, most of the newspaper
men were convinced as well as a rather high percentage of the more well-to-do farmers and some of the
labor union leaders. The left-wing farmers and the
left-wing leaders of union labor, however, never
believed in classical economics. They knew that large
corporations and tariffs had destroyed the validity
of its reasoning.

In summing up the effect of the ideas which have
made the United States, we can see how a hard-work-
ing, saving people have accumulated capital which
has been used to set machines ingeniously to work to
turn out increasing quantities of goods under a
doctrine of "competition unlimited." The people
have largely discarded a belief in the supernatural
and a future life from which source they originally
obtained much of their driving power. The competitive urge of the game has been used to some extent
as a substitute but it has not proved altogether satisfactory. Disillusionment is beginning to appear and

the fault essentially is with the nature of the ideas
which have dominated the minds of the American
people. What can we expect of the future?

The Dominating Ideas of the Future

The dominant political idea of the future will
probably have to do with the discovery of more
adequate methods of attaining unity in diversity.
To some extent this is the same political idea as the
Founding Fathers wrestled with during the period of
the Confederation and which in 1782 they inscribed
on the Great Seal with the Latin phrase "E pluribus
unum." Today because of the tremendous changes
wrought by new inventions, corporations, and the
shift of our population to the great cities, we find it
necessary to examine the idea in a fresh manner. The
Constitution of the United States endeavors to establish the idea of unity amidst diversity, but in
action certain parts of our national life have often
prospered at the expense of the whole because the
checks and balances which were designed to prevent
tyranny have been turned to selfish advantage.
These checks and balances have been of such nature
that we have found it necessary to throw them over-
board in every time of great emergency. Only a very
rich nation singularly strong and singularly isolated
can maintain its unity in triumph over so many
checks and balances. Our system employed by any
great mature nation in Europe would result in very
rapid disaster.

The totalitarian or corporative state represents

the ultimate in unity but it also represents the loss
of democratic privileges which we hold so dear.

It seems to me that the unity which we are seeking
has to do with evolving a concept of the general welfare grounded in both political and economic democracy. Can economic mechanisms be found which will
enable all of us over a great continent to work not
only for our own ends but for the general welfare?
Can a political mechanism be perfected which will
cause both the States and the three branches of the
Federal Government to take into account more
effectively the economic national welfare in all their
actions? Can this be done without losing the personal
privileges and liberties which we prize as the essence
of democracy? In economic matters it would seem
necessary that there would be increasing discipline on
behalf of the general welfare. When a nation becomes
mature there are certain types of economic liberty
which cannot be tolerated any more than automobile
drivers can be allowed to disobey a red light. Business leaders have sensed this necessity for some
time, and in the critical spring months of 1933 most
of them were willing to experiment in this direction.
The NRA taught us a great deal about policies which
will work and policies which will not work under our
form of government. The outstanding business men
of tomorrow will be those who develop a better mechanism which will enable the warring classes and
regions to work together in the interest of the general
welfare.

With all the increasing emphasis on unity and interdependence which seems to me to be inevitable during the next thirty years, it should not be forgotten that human welfare and happiness can only be expressed through individuals. Individuals, however, can learn to find joy in each other and in community of effort and not merely by competitive strife. The unity of the future must call to the limit on the creative faculties of the component parts of the social mechanism.

There must be the fullest possible development of the individual not merely in his own right but also in terms of the opportunities which the welfare of the whole affords. There can be a combination of socially desirable results with all that is constructive and creative in each individual.

In the economic world it is inevitable that more and more emphasis is going to be laid on the idea of co-operation as distinguished from free competition. The only way in which democracy can survive the logical onslaught of the dictator-state aspect of Communism and Fascism is to develop the genuine co-operative ideal to the limit. Producers' co-operatives are not enough. For the most part they merely take the place of middle men, and while in many cases they save a substantial part of the middle man's profit for the producer, they do not have any very profound effect on the people whom they serve. The co-operative way of life must pervade the community, and this means there must be consumers' co-operatives as well as producers' co-operatives. To live happily in a co-operative society takes an entirely different attitude of mind than that required in a society where free competition is the dominating rule. It is my belief that the hereditary nature of man is as well adapted to one order of society as the other. In fact, I am inclined to think that by nature most men are a little better adapted to the co-operative form of society than to the competitive form. The primitive co-operative forms of society as among the American Indians, for instance, prove how readily the nature of man adapts itself to the community co-operative approach. Such primitive types of community co-operation do not, it is true, provide very successfully for the "general welfare" in terms of a high standard of material living because they are so limited in their scope. They cannot accumulate capital and develop enterprise on a broad enough scale to raise the standard of living. The inadequacy of primitive co-operative forms in the economic world is freely admitted but it seems to me they prove beyond doubt that the "inherited nature" of man as distinguished from the "tradition-molded nature" of man is as much adapted to the co-operative as to the competitive way of life.

As a matter of fact, our modern capitalistic society is necessarily "co-operative" now, in one sense of the word. Much more than a primitive handicraft society, it has developed division of labor and specialization of skill, so that a highly interdependent relationship of economic groups is at the very heart of our

economic life. No man, whether on the assembly line
of an automobile factory or at the wheel of a farm
tractor or at the board of directors' table of a great
corporation, can live unto himself. As contrasted
with this basic interdependence, the competitive aspect of our society is to a large extent superficial. As
competitors we may forget the extent to which we are
all literally dependent on the labors of thousands of
other people; we may try to grab as much as we can
of the stream of money and things which come our
way; but the stream would dry up almost overnight
if it were not for the thousands and millions of people
who are merging their individual efforts to keep it
flowing. More than ever, now, we need to realize this
essential co-operative basis of modern society; we
need consciously to understand and work in har-
mony with the laws of interdependence. When our
minds have truly recognized these laws, when our
motives have become primarily co-operative and
only incidentally competitive, we can make our
individual labor count many times more effectively
than now in bringing to full fruitfulness the wealth-
producing and wealth-distributing possibilities of
our modern world.

The philosophy of the future will endeavor to
reconcile the good which is in the competitive, individualistic, and libertarian concepts of the nineteenth
century with the co-operative concepts which seem
to me destined to dominate the late twentieth
century.

My friend George W. Russell (AE), the Irish poet

and economic statesman who died in July of 1935, thought more effectively in this field than any one I know. In 1912 writing for Ireland, he made the following observations about the co-operative form of life which to my mind are fundamental and enduring:

Our co-operative associations in Ireland, gathering more and more into themselves the activities connected with production, consumption, and distribution, and even the social activities, as they grow more comprehensive in their aims, make the individual more conscious year by year that his interests are identical with the interests of the community. If it succeeds, he shares in its prosperity; and it is this spirit of mutual interdependence and comradeship in life, continually generated and maintained and inbred into the people, which is the foundation on which a great State, a great humanity, a beautiful civilization, can be built. The co-operative associations, properly constituted and organized, alone in modern times are capable of creating this spirit. Individualism in life or business can never create it. I never felt, so far, in any exposition of State Socialism which I have come across, that the writers had any understanding of social psychology, or by what means life may react on life so as to evoke brotherhood and public spirit. Understanding of economics apart from life there often was, and a passion for a mechanical justice, but I, at least, always feel that humanity under State control would be in a cul de sac. But it is quite possible to create without revolution, and by an orderly evolution of society within the State—not controlled by the State, but finally controlling its necessary activities— a number of free associations of workers and producers which, in the country, would have the character of small nations, and in the towns, of the ancient guilds, which would, I believe, produce more beauty, happiness and comfort than the gigantic mediocrity which always is the result of State activity. The Co-operative Commonwealth is the fourth alternative to State Socialism, the Servile State, or our present industrial anarchy; and Irishmen must make up their minds which of the four alternatives they prefer. They will be driven by the forces working in society to one or other of these courses. If capital wins we shall have the Servile State, and an immeasurable bureaucracy to keep the populace in order. If State Socialism wins humanity will have placed all its hopes on one system, and genius, temperament, passion, all the infinite variety of human life, will be constrained by one policy. Our present system is anarchic and inhuman, and the world is hurrying away from it with disgust. The Co-operative Commonwealth alone of all these systems allows freedom and solidarity. It allows for personal genius and unhampered local initiative. It develops a true sense of citizenship among its members. Whatever alternative Irishmen choose to promote they should think long and dispassionately on the prospects for humanity which each offers, and consider well their varying political, social and economic possibilities.*

The vision of a co-operative commonwealth which meant so much to Russell in 1912 was to some extent shattered by the terrible forces of the World War which he saw would sweep the world with passion

* *Co-operation and Nationality*, George Russell, published by Maunsel and Company, Dublin, 1912.

and confusion and therefore with desire for national
unity for many decades. In 1915 he foresaw the
inevitability of the increasing power of the State
(that is, the national government), and predicted
that by 1940, "there will hardly be anybody so
obscure, so isolated in his employment, that he will
not, by the development of the organized State, be
turned round to face it and to recognize it as the most
potent factor in his life. From that it follows of
necessity that literature will be concerned more and
more with the shaping of the character of this Great
Being. In free democracies, where the State inter-
feres little with the lives of men, the mood in literature tends to become personal and subjective; the
poets sing a solitary song about nature, love, twilight,
and the stars; the novelists deal with the lives of private persons, enlarging individual liberties of action
and thought. Few concern themselves with the
character of the State. But when it strides in, an
omnipresent overlord, organizing and directing life
and industry, then the individual imagination must
be directed to that collective life and power. For one
writer to-day concerned with high politics we may
expect to find hundreds engaged in a passionate attempt to create the new god in their own image.

"This may seem a far-fetched speculation, but not
to those who see how through the centuries humanity
has oscillated like a pendulum betwixt opposing
ideals. The greatest reactions have been from soli-

darity to liberty and from liberty to solidarity. The coming solidarity is the domination of the State."*

His statements both of 1912 and of 1915 have in them much of the prophetic. We all recognize their truth and beauty, and marvel at Russell's discernment of things to come. Every nation now hungers for an expression of national unity or solidarity but the only way in which that can be attained without sacrifice of the democratic theories of the rights of man is by building up the co-operative commonwealth. The building of a co-operative commonwealth in the United States raises of course much more difficult problems than are offered by a country such as George Russell's Ireland, where great accumulations of capital and machinery do not dominate the economic life, but where most people live in small rural or semi-rural communities. In the United States it is obvious that we cannot have a co-operative commonwealth without dealing with the question of our great industries which make up the chief part of our economic life. Unquestionably some means must be found by which these industries may operate more and more according to the needs of society and less on the basis of control by a few individuals for purposes of profit to the relatively few. As such means are found, it will be possible for more of our people to live in a way which enables the

* *Imaginations and Reveries*, George Russell, published by Macmillan and Company, Ltd., London, 1915.

individual to perform the task he is best fitted for while at the same time he may take pleasure in the knowledge that he is truly serving the general welfare. As it is now too many of us have to perform tasks and are forced at times to make decisions which, while they may temporarily advance our own interests, are not in accord with the general welfare.

In these concluding pages, I should like to draw attention to some of the brighter aspects of a future society based on co-operative rather than individualistic ideas, in the hope of persuading some of our more determined individualists that not all they cherish in the past way of life would be lost, and that something actually might be gained.

Capitalism while financially stronger today than ever before is becoming more and more spiritually bankrupt. It is because of this spiritual bankruptcy that capitalism under the stress of certain foreign situations has been replaced by economic dictatorships of several different types which carry with them the suppression of democratic safeguards. Both the Communist and Fascist approaches from a spiritual point of view seem to me to have many of the same difficulties as Capitalism. All three are largely the product of the British economics of the early nineteenth century and the post-Darwinian biology with their emphasis on an abstract "economic man" and an animalistic biological man, dominated by purely mechanical responses. Spiritually the result of the economic and biologic doctrines of

the nineteenth century was to exalt materialism and
to move the "Other Worldly" concepts of Protestantism, Catholicism and Judaism completely into
the background. Capitalism, Communism and Fascism all act as though there were no other end of
man than materialistic advancement. Life must be
devoted to something more inspiring than the
competitive search for profits, or the worship of the
materialistic dialectic or saluting one particular race
or nation as the quintessence of all that is, and therefore deserving of that emotional and intellectual
allegiance which Christians, Jews and Moham-
medans have hitherto reserved for God.

In searching for a spiritual power which will
operate in the world of practical affairs we find it
necessary, however, to take into account the realities of Capitalism, Fascism and Communism. One
of my critics urges that it is as appropriate for
America today to give concrete practical embodi-
ment to the doctrines of Marx and Lenin as it was
for the Founding Fathers to give concrete embodi-
ment to the ideas of Locke and Montesquieu in the
Declaration of Independence and the Constitution.
The argument is that just as the Founding Fathers
gave the European ideas of the eighteenth century a
pronounced American flavor so we today could well
use again philosophical ideas which have caused and
are likely to cause serious European bloodshed in
such a way as to enable them to work out benefi-
cently on this continent. Perhaps my critic is right

but somehow I like to think that the United States from now on will find developing naturally out of her own soil and her own people the spiritual and philosophic motive power of the future. In so far as our problems are the same as the overseas problems, and in so far as other nations, because they are older, have gained experience which should be of service to us there is every reason for studying that which they have learned. We are a part of the human race and cannot stand completely apart from any profound spiritual or philosophic doctrine.

If we do draw any inspiration direct or indirect from Marx, such inspiration will certainly be modified to fully as great an extent in practical operation as the Founding Fathers modified the Revolutionary French ideas in working out the Constitution.

For my own part I believe the United States is now sufficiently mature in her economic and political experience so that she will increasingly serve as the source of spiritual, philosophic and political ideas which will furnish motive power not only for our own future, but for the entire world.

The society of the future, it seems to me, will not only emphasize the co-operative welfare as contrasted with individualistic competition, but it will emphasize life as contrasted with mechanics. The scientists and inventors of the past 150 years have found the analytical, mathematical and mechanical approach most valuable. By specializing, every man was able to know more and more about less and less and the process seemed to pay. But in the twentieth century, it has been discovered that there is something about living things and especially about human beings which defies this approach. Human personality resists abstraction; our scientists may dissect life in the laboratory until a tremendous collection of minute data has been gathered, but as long as each bit is made an end in itself all of it is dead. Their research can come to life again only if the parts are seen as a living whole. Not forgetting analysis and precise measurement, I believe in the future we will study life more as function and relationship than as individual form.

Our biological and physical scientists are also beginning to see that many of their discoveries are academic or even destructive as long as they cannot be fitted into a general social scheme which can take advantage of them. Dietitians may provide us with extremely useful knowledge of how people may live more healthful lives, diseases be prevented and human beings made more efficient and happy, but as long as half of our people cannot afford the diets they suggest, their information is relatively unusable. Inventors may give us more and more cunning mechanical devices for saving human energy and time, but as long as these discoveries result chiefly in the involuntary leisure of unemployment, they do not add to the sum of human happiness. A co-operative society should be able to take these discoveries from the theoretical sphere of the laboratory or from the profit-controlled sphere of business competition, and place them in a functional relation to human welfare. With the mechanical elements of research and discovery put in their proper perspective, many of our students and scientists could turn their attention to the ends of human life rather than merely the means.

Artistic expression and appreciation, the freeing of the creative urge in human beings, pleasure in nature, the joy of contemplation will have a much wider place in the society of the future. The original philosophy of Protestantism was grim. Man was laboring under the burden of original sin from which he could escape by the skin of his teeth if he worked hard every minute of the day and God looked on him with favor in the closing seconds of his life. Art, beauty and sex were looked upon with suspicion. Americans as a whole have largely abandoned this grim philosophy. During the decade after the war there was a wild reaction against restraint by "flaming youth" and their heavily drinking parents. This revolt of the '20s was based on escape from reality rather than in true pleasure in reality; young people and many of their elders were trying to forget the horror and disillusion of the war and avoid facing the problems it had created. Since the early '20s many of our young people have revolted once more, and have become stern and rather humorless reformers, impatient with their elders in a different way. No doubt this is much to the good. Meanwhile, however, artistic expression suffers when our more talented people are preoccupied with economic doctrines and struggles. While this may be necessary for the time being, a broad cultural life can flourish only when we have achieved a more secure society, in which the human spirit can be more largely released from questions of immediate livelihood.

Where Are We Now?

I have said that the co-operative philosophy is the vital idea of the twentieth century that is bound to translate itself in time into the hard facts of social mechanisms and reality. But how is this to come about? What is the relation in time between a moral concept and a social mechanism? The moral concept of the rights of man was translated into political action by American political realists at the end of the eighteenth century. A number of circumstances combined to make the transformation possible. But paramount was the fact that enough enlightened men had become so saturated and stimulated with the idea that when the circumstances arose, they could create the mechanisms needed to clothe the idea with reality.

No one can say just when circumstances in our day will be such that the co-operative idea can be clothed in appropriate social mechanisms. Already some advance has been made; in the last three years we have learned a great deal about the mechanics of co-operation, and what we have learned should stand us in good stead. I think, for example, of the county committees of farmers who under the AAA were responsible for the actual carrying out of the programs in the field, and who, under the new program, are again the focal point of economic democracy for agriculture. Meanwhile, nothing is more important than that more and more people become actively imbued with the idea of a co-operative society.

Let us take a leaf from the book of our forefathers, those bold political realists whom I have called the wise young men of 1787. Their confidence in action grew out of the moral certainty that their purposes were in line with the stream of destiny of their time. They were not a very large group in mere numbers; in fact, they were probably greatly outnumbered by the others who did not agree with their particular proposals or were apathetic. Unquestionably the great majority of people did believe in the general spirit of the new ideas; in democracy, freedom and the rights of man. But the young men who pressed for adoption of the Constitution knew they could not expect unanimity to develop of itself with respect to the particular political forms and social mechanisms by which these general ideas could be realized. The best they could do was to initiate proposals, provide for discussion and reconciliation of conflicting points of view, and then, by the reasonableness of their argument and the eloquence of their conviction, hope to convince a majority of people that their program should be adopted.

They went up and down the country carrying the gospel of their new program. In *The Federalist*, they erected a brilliant forum for argument and persuasion concerning it. It required almost a year to convince enough people to insure adoption of the Constitution, and without the determined campaign of the group of men who believed deeply in its principles, the whole enterprise would undoubtedly have been lost.

The cue for solution of our present problems lies in the Constitution itself, in its declaration of the united purpose of the people, through government, to deal with the eternal problems of justice, liberty and the general welfare. These problems take new forms; previous mechanisms may not suffice to meet them. New concepts of how to approach them arise in a new age. It would be contrary to the very spirit in which the men of 1787 acted to shrink from the task of realizing appropriate means for promoting the general welfare today. The Constitution itself was the product of a deep conviction that instruments of government are devised by men for furthering the welfare of men, that they have no other purpose or reason for being. Not to use the Constitution in that spirit, but to set it up as a sacred and changeless authority on changing material conditions, is to deny the kernel and worship the husk.

Today we need a great many more persons who will become as deeply motivated by the idea of a cooperative economic society as the young men of 1776 and 1787 were motivated by the idea of a democratic political society. The one is the living stream of thought for the twentieth century as the other was for the eighteenth. I believe the majority of American people are already receptive to the general purposes and possibilities of a co-operative commonwealth. They want more security in sickness, in old age, in unemployment; they want a wider distribution of the good things of life; and they have become disillusioned of the system, in its present self-contradicting form, of free-competition-and-devil-take-the-hindmost as a method for reaching those ends. The prevalence of various over-simple schemes and movements for achieving such ends is indicative of the feeling of many people. The need is for a body of people in accord on general aims, as idealistic and as realistic as were the young Federalists of 1787, to channelize thought and initiate and consider proposals which may lead to a co-operative society. The means for conveying ideas are certainly more extensive than they were in the 1780's, even though there are 30 times as many people to reach. Perhaps the very multiplicity of means makes for confusion. But we may well profit by the example of the young men of 1787 who used *The Federalist* with such effect, in utilizing similar national forums for analyzing and propagating new proposals. By such means, by the give-and-take of discussion, by the determined effort of persons themselves convinced and thus able to convince others, new concepts will eventually take form in social mechanisms.

It seems to me that thoughtful people today, in relation to prospective action, stand somewhat in the position of thoughtful men in the early 1780's. At that time they were increasingly aware that the set-up under the Articles of Confederation was not working out to meet national problems in an adequate way. They were thinking, suggesting, comparing ideas and plans, wondering what action was necessary, wondering what form it should take, whether the Articles needed amendment, revision or what. They had not got to the point of actually formulating a definite plan.

Similarly, thoughtful people today are wondering what action will be needed. They know that solution of our present problems will eventually require a new kind of statecraft as effective in the economic field as was the statecraft of Madison, Hamilton and the others in the more purely political field. The precise form of statecraft which will be required, however, does not yet appear. Thoughtful people today believe that the Constitution provides ample scope for evolution toward the new form of statecraft. Much depends, however, on the way the Constitution is interpreted and on the way old or new legislation under the Constitution is used by pressure groups. Much depends on whether the plain intent of the Constitution to enable government to promote the general welfare can really be effectuated under modern economic conditions. If this book has shown anything, it has shown that the present relationships of economic groups and the present scope of individual and governmental action do not work out sufficiently toward the general welfare. If it raises any question of immediate concern to all of us, it is: Who owns the Constitution, if not the people as a whole?

If our more privileged and powerful people under the present rules of the game—financiers, corporation lawyers and directors—resolutely fail to understand the signs of the times, one type of statecraft may need to be evolved. If they are alive to the necessity for making certain fundamental changes in order to preserve the general welfare quite a different form of statecraft may be in order. One situation might eventually require amendments to the Constitution. Another might require nothing in the way of constitutional changes. In various countries of the world in the past, privileged classes have often acted in such a way as to make gradual change impossible and have precipitated violent action. Some countries, as for example Sweden, have shown a capacity for gradual change, and have made steady progress in the direction of co-operative organization and intelligent social action.

We in the United States should eventually be prepared if necessary to work out in the spirit of Madison a mechanism which would embody the spirit of the age as successfully as the Constitution of 1787 mirrored the philosophy of the eighteenth century. We may hope that such action can be taken as bloodlessly as the Constitution was enacted and that the handiwork will be as enduring. This will un-doubtedly be possible if a spirit of common sense prevails;—and if we use our Constitution as Hamilton anticipated it should be used, such action may not be necessary at all.*

America's contribution in 1787 to world governmental practice was enormously significant. It is my belief that in the spirit, if not in the form of 1787, the United States can, in the not too distant future, make again fully as great a contribution to the productivity and ordered welfare of the peoples of the world and perhaps an even greater contribution to the consuming power and happiness of all the nations.

* See Article 34 of *The Federalist*, as quoted on page 205 of this book.

Index